Cordillera

-Literature from the World's Toughest Bike Race-

Founding Editor

Eric A. Bruntjen

For when you
get 5 minutes to have a read!
Happy fathers day
2011
Oliver
xxx

Special Thanks to

Lucy Bruntjen, Melanee Bruntjen

Eric Bruntjen, Editor

www.thecordillera.org

thecordillera@gmail.com

Volume 1, June 2010

Cover Photo Top by Aaron Teasdale

Cover Photo Bottom by Eddie Clark

Back Cover GDMBR Graphic courtesy of the Adventure Cycling Association

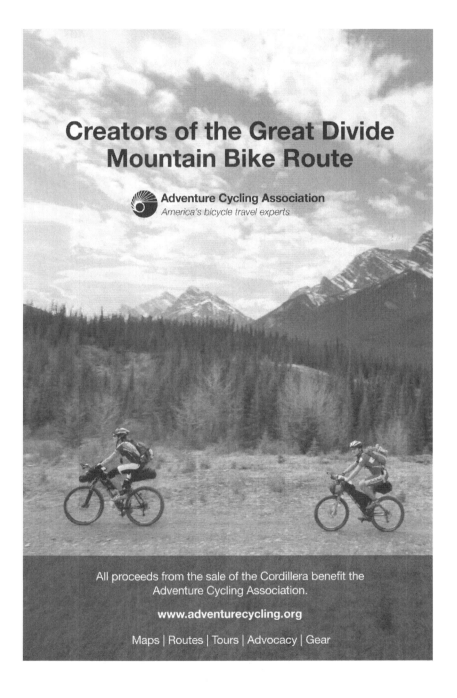

Table of Contents

Divide Racing \də-'vīd\ \rās-ing\

The Race: Divide Racing is a single stage, unsupported, off-pavement bicycle time trial for individual cyclists. The race follows the Great Divide Mountain Bike Route (GDMBR) as described by the Adventure Cycling Association.

The Route: Great Divide Mountain Bike Route (GDMBR) closely follows the geographic Continental Divide from Canada to Mexico. The route is mountainous and remote with many portions being several hundred miles from civilization. The 2,745 mile long route is characterized by unpredictable weather and difficult cycling terrain.

The Events: Although Divide Racing is an individual affair, two loosely organized events characterize the sport: the Tour Divide, which launches from Banff, Canada, follows the entire 2,745 mile GDMBR route while the original Great Divide Race (GDR) begins in Port of Rooseville, Montana and runs solely within the United States. Both races end on the southern border of the United States at Antelope Wells, New Mexico.

History: Both races seek to emulate John Stamstad's legendary 1999 solo time trial of the route. Mike Curiak, creator of the GDR, is considered to be the architect of Divide Racing's group start while Matthew Lee is recognized for including the Canadian segment of the GDMBR the Tour Divide.

Miscellaneous: Both races are known for "call-ins" in which racers leave detailed messages on their location and current condition. The recordings are then posted to the Internet for the benefit of race fans. The Tour Divide also employs SPOT satellite locators which display racer positions, in near real time, on the race website.

Participants are known as Divide Racers. While attrition rates run as high as forty percent a successful Divide Racer may complete the race in three weeks or less, often cycling sixteen or more hours per day. Divide Racing is an individual sport for which there is no earthly compensation. However, many participants report that the prolonged physical and mental challenges provide for a deep spiritual reward.

See Also: www.tourdivide.org, www.greatdividerace.com, www.adventurecycling.org

About the Cordillera

When I flew home from participating in the 2009 Tour Divide race a stack of mail the size and shape of a fieldstone column was waiting for me. In that pile, buried under the usual dregs of a middle class existence, were some glossy old friends whom I'd missed out on the trail: *The New Yorker, The Atlantic Monthly* and *The Paris Review*.

Over the next few days I read the whole stack and thought about the comedy, drama and tragedy that Divide Racers live with on the long trail south. Was there, I wondered, a way to compile those stories into a respectable collection? To make a long story short the answer I came to was "No."

It wasn't that I thought of my fellow Divide Racers as incapable or untalented, quite the opposite. I was simply worried that they would be too busy living an adventurous life to stop and write about it. The two worlds seemed infinitely far apart

So I shelved the project and moved on to other things like trying to get the feeling back in my fingertips, something my race along The Divide had robbed me of.

But then a copy of *The Whitefish Review* showed up. The Review is published on the edge of Glacier National Park by a group of friends who write, drink beer, ski and fish, especially fish. The editors of The Review are creative outlaws who smell like trout -imagine Johnny Cash in hip waders- and they have been successfully tweaking naysayers for a couple of years now. Their standards are high (too high to accept a submission of mine last summer) and they've thrived in a marketplace where industry veterans have recently gone toes up. If there's proof that adventurous, mountain people can also love words and books it's *The Whitefish Review*.

Cordillera

After thumbing through *The Whitefish Review* it became clear that my inspiration for a Divide Racing literature review should not come from affected prose but rather the "Hey check this out" enthusiasm of Whitefish, Montana; itself a pit stop on The Divide. Shortly thereafter an email went out and the submissions started rolling in.

It turns out that Divide Racers and fans of the sport are generous people because they quickly replied with enthusiasm. They are darn good writers too. Good enough for even *The Whitefish Review*? I certainly think so, but we'll never know because the authors featured here chose the Cordillera and that means a lot. Thank you submitters!

The goal of the Cordillera is not to give rote testimony to the twists and turns of the Great Divide Mountain Bike Route. Nor is it our desire to document the records that, amazingly, seem to fall every year. Rather it exists to lend a polished voice to the spirit of The Divide and those who race on it. To get in the Cordillera a piece must have heart and a compelling story. Two things that The Divide has no shortage of.

Eric Bruntjen —editor

2010

The Moral Predicament of Begging for Food
(And living to tell your Mom about it.)

Cadet Bryant

In her book *Writing the Memoir*, Judith Barrington says that, "To write honestly about our lives requires that we work at and refine our artistic skills so that our memoirs can effectively communicate the hard-won, deep layers of truth that are rarely part of conventional social discourse. It requires, too, that we grapple with all the ethical questions that arise when we shun commonly accepted definitions of loyalty: questions like, 'Can I really tell that story or will it hurt my mother?'"

In the spring of 2009, my dear, sweet Mom dropped me off at the airport to catch a flight to Calgary, Canada, for the Tour Divide Race—a 2,745-mile mountain bike epic (ranked as one of the hardest off-road races on the planet) that extends from Banff, Alberta, to Antelope Wells, New Mexico. One of the last things she said to me was, "Promise me that you won't put yourself in the position of having to beg for food while you're out there. Do you know how to catch a squirrel? . . . Make sure you should get a knife in case you need to skin something, and then all ya' gotta' do is roast it on a fire."

The Tour Divide is tough on Mothers and mine wasn't the only one worried about her son. Another racer's Mom told him: "Don't do anything stupid like try and win. I don't want you to kill yourself!"

On the third day of the race, a torturous one-hundred-and-twenty-five-mile stretch of no-man's-land between Sparwood, British Columbia, and Eureka, Montana, I was already in trouble and scanning for squirrels along the trail. After sixteen hours of climbing out of the Canadian Rockies, all the food I had eaten was a piece of fried chicken with some soggy fries and a handful of jelly beans. I was bonking hard with no good prospect for an honorable restocking of food. I knew that any store or restaurant I passed would most likely be closed at that late hour and I realized that begging for food was probably in my near future.

~Mom, I'm sorry, but the rest of this story may hurt you... I did, in fact, beg for food.~

I had no choice, I felt like I was going to pass out; my head swam and my swollen knees wobbled as they slowly cranked the pedals southward. When I finally reached the outskirts of Eureka, well after dark, I stopped at the first sign of civilization: an RV campground, and shamelessly begged for food.

I knocked loudly on a camper door and stepped back when an old man cracked open the door. "Yeah?" he said.

"Sir, please . . . I need food. Anything you've got . . . Please. I'll take anything."

I saw it in his eyes, *Who is this moron?* He pointed down the road and said, "Go 'bout a mile further and there's a restaurant that stays open late on the left. Beg for food there." Slam! I felt lucky he hadn't shot me through the thin aluminum door and decided not to risk begging from any more of the darkened campers.

A mile further was a lifetime, but I made it and soon stood in front of a group of locals drinking beer on a restaurant porch. I begged there too but they couldn't understand a word I was saying. Was it my West Texas accent? Was I slurring my speech? Was I too tired and hungry to work my own jaw? I eventually just spit it out—the most basic, simple, verbal telegraph: "Food. Please. Food!"

They understood that!

A lady on the dark side of the porch took a swig of beer and said, "I closed down the grill an hour ago, but if you go four more miles down the road you'll get to the main part of town and you'll see the VFW . . . Go in there, beg again, and some old men will make you a hamburger."

~ Beg again? Oh Mom, will you ever forgive me? ~

I still don't know how I made it to town. All I remember is that the lights were off at the VFW and that I was afraid of being the first Divide Racer to die of outright starvation.

Just down from the VFW, I found the only thing still open in Eureka, Montana, at 11:00 at night—an Exxon gas station. I rambled in and started swiping things off the shelves . . . Anything that my eyes landed on was stuffed into my mouth: Twinkies, Ho-Ho's, donuts, Doritos, milk, Twix bars . . . I was a madman, mauling anything that came

9

my way. Cellophane be damned, if it didn't open on the first tear, I stuffed the whole package in my mouth.

The attendant was silent until I approached the counter –bloated and white as biscuit dough. "Uh . . . You know, if you're really *that* hungry, I can make you something on the grill." Manna from heaven, or at least from a small town Fry Cook.

"I'll take twenty dollars worth of anything please," I mumbled while spitting crackers and Fig Newtons down the front of my jersey.

The next morning I pulled out of the race with unbearable knee pain. It was hard but there's no shame in scratching from the world's toughest bike race. I gave my all and honored the ethos of Divide Racing by cycling well and respecting the rules. In *A River Runs through It*, Norman Maclean writes that ". . . If our father had had his say, nobody who did not know how to fish would be allowed to disgrace a fish by catching him."

~ Mom, I'm sorry that I had to beg for food out there in the wild, but while I was on top of the last mountain on Day Three, just above the Montana border, shivering, and weeping for food, I wouldn't allow myself to catch a squirrel because . . . well, I would have disgraced him. ~

Everyman's GDR

Jon Billman

I needed the inertia of a race. My tendency is toward touring, slowly, smelling the hop flowers, and with that approach I'd still be on the Continental Divide, reading a book in my tent, eating tacos, maybe drinking a beer. I recall Frisco, Colorado, where the Great Divide Route transects the Trans America Route. Outside the grocery store I met a young man touring on a sleek road racing bike. His bike was clean and shiny as he was. His name was Jon, spelled like my name, and he was with what appeared to be half a dozen pretty medical students from the University of Georgia. This pelotonic harem wore matching stretchy kits, their calves were smooth and tan, they were going to be doctors and they were hitting every brew pub on the route, coast to coast, and invited me to join them at this idyllic joint on a corner in historic Frisco. Did they not understand I was in a race? I wanted to join them—did I ever—but the duty of the GDR bid me to decline. These fresh southerners and their leisurely approach and pace!—well, that's my typical speed.

I did not have the time away from family or work to afford me such a trip, so if I wanted to ride the Divide—America's spiritual, geographical and geological vertebrae—I had to muster into the Great Divide Race. And what could be better than a self-supported race with no entry fee, no qualifying times, no real rules and no prizes? Imagine trying to line up at the Tour de France on race day. The GDR is egalitarian. American. IMHO, the Last Great Race. I'm slow, but I will be racing! Money is not a motivation for these riders and their relatively low-tech mounts. Sponsorships? Sponsors are into flash and cameras, not an athlete at large in the desert like a chapter out of Exodus. Go ahead and cheat—it's your own damn self that'll you'll have to live with for the rest of your life.

A 2009 Tour Divide Racer. Copyright Eddie Clark.

Blame Kenny Maldonado for my GDR obsession. Kenny showed up in Whitefish with his tankish Specialized Enduro and enormous rucksack in June of 2006. The wrenches at Glacier Cyclery like to tell the story of how they insisted he get rid of the Coleman items from his pack that were weighing him down—he'd leave the start line with only 50 pounds of gear instead of 80. When he slowly rolled into the Great Divide Basin, where there are no pay phones, no gas stations, most often no water, he disappeared from the race's "radar," the GDR website. Matthew Lee was way out in front by this time, but they were the only two riders left in the race. Even though Matthew was fighting suspension fork problems, I did not have to worry about him, but I'd become emotionally invested in Kenny. He was Everycyclist and probably, like me, made *vroom! vroom!* sounds when he pedaled. He was in the GDR to see wildlife. To get under the weather. Maybe to meet himself. Call it a midlife crisis, whatever that is, but I knew the GDR would be a watershed moment— har har har—in my life like I suspect it was in Kenny's. He didn't make the race past the Greyhound station in Rawlins, but I have no doubt he dieseled back to New York a more interesting person. If Matthew Lee had decided to abandon the GDR in 2006, Kenny Maldonado, this dude from the Big Apple, might have won. If "ifs" and "buts" were candy and nuts Kenny might have feasted his way to a slow, albeit legitimate, victory. But it's those "ifs" and "buts" that make the GDR so damn fascinating: a real race.

I trained in the flatlands of Oklahoma, Kansas and Iowa (strangely, my favorite training rides would take me through the Des Moines River valley near Boone, Iowa, where Mac McCoy, author of Cycling the Divide, grew up). I read Mac's guidebook cover-to-cover a dozen times as if it were a good novel. My buddy John Hunsaker—I call him Ham—is a renowned triathlon coach at the USA Triathlon Training Center in Burlington, Iowa. Ham gave me a lactic acid threshold test and designed a target heart rate zone workout program for me that involved countless hours on exercycles in wintry Iowa gyms. He had to have had doubts about my success on the GDR, but then tri-athletes are notoriously unbalanced characters themselves.

Motivational coaches will tell you to share your goals with others. This is different than bragging, of course, but a funny thing I found when I needed another gear on, say, Indiana Pass in southern Colorado—I didn't want to go back and explain to people that I'd *almost* made it to Antelope Wells; for me a partial GDR would be worse than no GDR—I could have used those thousands of hours of training and obsessing for other things. I'd pedal like a lab rat and envision climbing and descending the 200,000 vertical feet of the Great Divide. Was it possible to train in Iowa and race the length of the Rockies? I wasn't sure. I took heart in this: Ham instructed me that it's better to be fifty percent undertrained than to be twenty percent over-trained. I could be that! I'd show up in Port Roosville exceptionally undertrained. Matthew Lee gave me this advice to boot: "You can race your way into shape."

I became obsessed. Work and workouts made me cranky and my wife Hilary was nothing short of selfless. My kids thought I was either out on my bike or on the couch "being lazy." Everything became a piece of the GDR puzzle. I gave up drinking and found I didn't really miss my evening beer, that three aspirin and bed would do the trick. When I was too tired to move I'd check equipment or order some new thing, a nostrum; the UPS man showed up almost daily. In May I drove to Emporia, Kansas with my friend Paul Jacobson and rode the Dirty Kanza 200 and pulled the plug after 150. If I couldn't ride 200 miles of Kansas, how could I ride the 2,490 miles along the spine of the Rocky Mountains? I was insecure to be sure, but had become numb, a GDR zombie. It's funny how fatigue and momentum, underrated qualities in my experience, can trump self doubt.

The hardest part of the entire race was leaving the family at the crappy airport motel in Tulsa and getting on a small jet for Kalispell. But once on the ground I had work to do, and other racers like Matt McFee and Matt Kemp showed up and for the first time I felt a GDR camaraderie, a spirited dingy full of pedaling pilgrims. I had a bike to assemble, food to organize, maps to consult, and no time for hand wringing. The race is nonstop troubleshooting and thinking about logistics and nutrition, navigation and mechanics takes up any free hard drive space, with just enough left to become superstitious. This isn't news to adventure cyclists, who do this on any remote trip, but the conceit of a race, a grand American one, intensifies everything.

If you find yourself thinking about the GDR, say, in the middle of the night, maybe keeping the GDR website on your computer's desktop at work and checking for call-ins from riders whom you've vicariously adopted instead of getting work done, well, you've been bitten, you'll develop an itchy rash and I'd urge you to take up bowling before the poison pollutes your bloodstream.

The Note on the Bottle

Felix Wong

If I hadn't already spent most of the day weaving around potholes deep enough to swallow a small vehicle, perhaps I would not have felt so anxious. If I hadn't already dismounted from my bicycle, climbed over fallen trees and remounted hundreds of times, maybe I would not have been so tired. Maybe, if I weren't all alone among the notoriously ill-tempered Grizzlies who live on Montana's Richmond Peak, I wouldn't have been so scared. In any case, I was all of those things and more on the fifth day of the 2008 Tour Divide, which is probably why I started talking to myself.

"I wish I had crampons and an ice axe," I muttered under my breath before giving in and screaming, "THIS... IS... NUTS!"

The sky had already started to turn scarlet from a setting sun, and I was on a perilous one-mile stretch of the northward-facing peak in Lolo National Forest. The road had been pummeled by avalanches all winter and stood buried under seven feet of snow at a frightening angle. To my left was a sheer, hundred foot drop-off. To my right was an un-scalable Jacob's Ladder of frozen snow. I muttered, out loud again, that without climbing gear it would only be a matter of time before I went skittering off the mountain like a skydiver falling out of an airplane.

If there were not deep tire tracks in the snow from racers who had gone before me, I would have thought this section impassable, that it could not possibly be part of the Great Divide Mountain Bike Route. But the tracks told me that it was, so I gingerly traversed the section by walking sideways and kicking steps into the snow while hoisting my bike up and slamming it down -the world's worst ice-ax. Over and over I repeated my absurd dance: kick, lift, slam and inch sideways. Repeat several hundred times and talk out loud; that's how you do the Richmond Peak Shuffle.

Just one misstep would have resulted in lost equipment, broken bones, or worse. At one point I moved my satellite-tracker off my bike and onto my shoulder. The vain hope was that, if I went down the cliff, my tracker would at least guide rescuers to my body before the bears arrived.

After a heart-pounding hour on what would come to be known among racers that year as the Traverse of Death, I found myself on solid ground again. There were still miles of snow-covered trail ahead but at least I didn't have to fret about tumbling off the precipice like a frozen Wile E. Coyote in spandex.

Before my nerves settled, an unnatural shape in the trail caught my eye. I stopped dead in my tracks, confused. "What's that?" I said, still talking out loud. Empty and splayed, the pile seemed ominous, almost body-like. A shiver rippled through my legs as I gulped down saliva and squinted. Had another racer died? "Probably of fright" I said, out loud to no one but me and the bears. One of whom, I realized, may have been responsible for the body-shaped pile ahead.

On closer inspection, I recognized the items as a GoLite brand jacket and a standard bicycle water bottle. The jacket was made from adobe-colored nylon -waterproof and wind-resistant. It was expensive and weighed less than a small banana. Like the jacket, the translucent bike bottle looked brand new.

What were they doing here?

At first I assumed that I wasn't alone, that another person was about, possibly relieving themselves in the woods. But as I looked around, I heard and saw no one. Then my thoughts turned to what terrible fate may have befallen the mysterious litterbug. Had the Divide Racer been attacked by a bear? Were they swallowed whole with only these items left behind? Or did they make a hasty escape and drop their expensive jacket as a clever distraction? Neither scenario seemed likely; the gear was intact, un-clawed and in pristine condition. I also saw no blood, body parts or other signs of a struggle with one of Richmond Peak's legendary bruins.

Was someone trying to shed weight? Possibly, considering how gram-obsessed most Divide Racers are. But to drop unwanted items would be littering and rude. I knew that couldn't be the answer. Divide Racers can be rude, but we don't litter!

Ultimately, I decided that Matthew Lee -the race leader and key organizer of the Tour Divide- had stashed the items to provide the hapless rear guard with survival gear on one of the most treacherous peaks in Montana. I didn't need the gear, but I thought that someone else might, so I scrawled a note about my theory and attached it to the bottle before moving on.

> *"Matt Lee probably left these for those who really need them on this crazy mtn!!! Good luck!! -Felix Wong, Tour Divide Racer, 21:25 6-17-08"*

I didn't give the items another thought until after the race when I learned that it was fellow racer Mike Dion who had lost the gear. His pack was overstuffed so he had to attach some items to the outside and somehow they worked themselves loose. Mike was disappointed to lose the bottle and especially the jacket, but later joked that they were sacrificial offerings to the Gods for safe passage along the Great Divide.

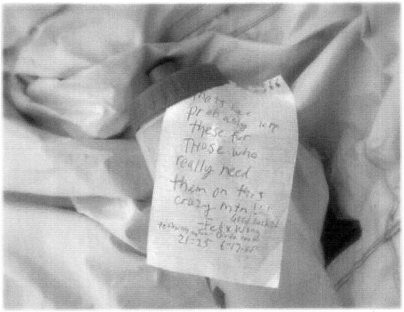

Copyright Felix Wong.

"I think if I would have thrown down a multi-tool for them I would have made it to the Mexican border," he said.

As it turned out, other racers who came through the area in the days afterward saw my scribbled musings and reached their own conclusions. Some thought that I had left the gear behind myself while others wondered if Matthew Lee was going to leave them food and water in the Great Basin, still a few thousand miles south. The note became my proverbial message in a bottle. To me it was just a letter thrown out onto a sea of Montana snow but to other racers it was a link, a ribbon of generosity linking us all on the Great Divide. The legend of my bottle was even carried over to the next year when the 2009 Tour Divide racers started keeping an eye out for "messages from Wong," on Richmond Peak. In hindsight I realize that I probably should have carried the gear to the next town and properly disposed of them there but who thinks clearly on Richmond Peak? At least I didn't carve "F.W. was here" on a tree!

Whatever ultimately happened to the jacket and water bottle, no one knows -perhaps a bear or an especially stylish yeti is using them to survive somewhere in the Lolo National Forest to this day.

Dispatches from the Great Basin

Eric Bruntjen

Of all the preparations I made for the 2009 Tour Divide race, my late night research sessions were the most self indulgent. Once a week I'd return from a hundred mile training ride, tuck my son into bed, smooch my ever-patient wife goodnight and fire up the computer to do a little obsessive Googling. For the rest of the night my low fat, high pain-in-the-ass diet was tossed out the window while I munched on quesadillas and gulped down frosty porters. As the evening wore on I'd burn up the Internet between my modest house in central Washington and anything related to the Tour Divide which, at almost 3,000 miles in length, is recognized as one of the world's toughest mountain bike races. During these late night sessions the race seemed to shrink a little; the very act of putting facts to fears was comforting. I learned, for example, that Indiana Pass is 11,950 feet high, that Hartsel, Colorado has more bars than grocery stores and that the current record holder, Mathew Lee, is a robot. These are all good things to know before attempting an unsupported off-road rampage, along the Continental Divide, from Banff, Canada to the Mexican border.

Of particular interest to me during these late night sessions was the Great Basin. A relatively flat and hot leg of the race, the Great Basin is described by geologists as "internally draining". Water that flows into the basin has a hard time getting out, which can also be said for Divide Racers. Although fully prepared for steep mountain passes, some racers find the endless rolling hills and sustained elevation in the basin to be unnerving and flag a bus home from Rawlins, Wyoming on the basin's southern edge.

Intrigued by the basin I did what any Tour Divide hopeful would do and revisited Jon Billman's 2008 *Outside Magazine* article, *The World's Toughest Bike Race Is Not in France*. The article was the inspiration for my own Tour Divide attempt and I found his blue collar "if I can do it so can you" prose invigorating. Jon used words like "alkaline" and "lawless" to describe the Great Basin which was itself a character in his article. In my mind the basin grew into a geological Boo Radley, a featureless watcher who drove the plot forward, always forward like the Tour Divide.

I was so inspired by the article that I used the same line on my wife as Jon had used on his.

"Make it me!" I sang to the love of my life, begging for her permission to race along the Continental Divide.

Melanee finally agreed but only after reading the dog eared article herself and being won over by its glossy call to arms. That was no small accomplishment; Melanee was pregnant at the time and due to give birth to our daughter only four months before the start of the Tour Divide. Consider also the fact that our firstborn son would be a rambunctious two year old when I left them all behind and you can reach an interesting conclusion: Jon Billman can talk anybody into anything.

In his article Jon wrote about the 2006 Great Divide Race when, as a fan, he followed Kenny Maldonado chase Matthew Lee southward through Montana, Idaho and Wyoming. Kenny put up a good fight until he was swallowed by the Great Basin only to emerge in Rawlins as a broken racer who called it quits at the Greyhound station. Kenny's old college try, his Gallipoli charge in the sage, was an inspiration for some but that's not how I saw it.

"Don't make that me!" I wheezed on training rides while thinking about Kenny and the Great Basin.

As the winter wore on my interest in the Great Basin grew into an obsession. I researched temperature, wind speed and terrain while building a detailed profile on the basin. I consulted topographic maps and even scanned a scientific paper or two but it was a waste of time. When I lined up at the start in Banff my plan for the Great Basin was little more than naïve chest thumping. I was going to put my boot on the neck of that nothingness and make it bend to my will. It seemed like a reasonable strategy but The Divide didn't play fair.

The day before I rolled into the Great Basin I hurt myself while fighting that infernal divide mud on Wyoming's Togwotee Pass. I was out of my gourd with frustration. I can't say exactly where the tendons in my right ankle spun into cotton candy but it may have been when I threw my 29er into the frozen meconium and trudged away on foot. I suppose my intention was to walk to Mexico but after a mile or two I stiffened my resolve and went back for the bike. I eventually dug deep and survived Togwotee but the damage was done and I ground to a halt again on nearby Union Pass.

That's where my guardian angel found me, a broken man only fractionally there, sitting on the steps of the Sawmill Lodge. The Lodge was still closed for the season but my angel rented a room to me anyway. Her name was Evi; she called me "sweetie" and sold me a plate of fruit. She put ice on my ankle and saved my race.

My memories of that night are like those of a man caught in a frantic nightmare; they are in the present tense and rambling.... *My ankle swells up to a cartoonish size and turns a shiny purple. I set the heater to full blast. The thermostat rotates past 75 but I'm freezing. I shiver under the covers and drag myself out of bed for a lumbering knee-walk to the bathroom. I fill the tub with steaming water and roll in. I fear that my race is over and pray for the first time in twenty years.*

The next morning there was no obvious miracle. If God had answered my prayers He'd only grudgingly done so. I could gingerly flex my purple ankle but after a few steps the pain flared and I sat down to consider throwing in the towel. It seemed like the smart thing to do; I could rationalize it easily enough. "You'll do permanent damage to your leg." I mumbled out loud.

But months before I had set a trap for myself that I just couldn't wiggle out of. Before starting the race, I had collected pledges to benefit Evan Mettie, a terribly injured Iraq War Veteran from my home town. The local newspaper had caught wind of the story and by the time I left for the race there were enough pledges to buy him a new motorized all terrain wheelchair, but only if I finished at Antelope Wells, New Mexico. The pledges were on a per mile basis. If I scratched on Union Pass there would be no chair, only the shame of an unfinished promise to a soldier and his family. Caught by my own device I had no choice but to limp out the front door, get back on my bike and inch toward the Great Basin.

The attraction of divide racing is difficult to explain because we all have our own vivid images of what a bike ride is. Forget that. The Tour Divide has nothing to do with bike paths, single track or pelotons. Sure, the race consists mostly of unromantic realities like crawling up logging roads and calorie management but there's another side to divide racing, a restorative side that in many ways is like music, hunting or sex, but writ large. It's about building then releasing tension –up a mountain and down a mountain, rain then sun, heartache followed by joy. In contrast, the modern world -with its non-slip surfaces and pre-packaged meat- is intent on avoiding tension. Off The Divide we are protected from extremes but it comes at a steep cost: our souls are trapped in a sexless marriage with the world.

Not on the Tour Divide. Out here plates get thrown and your underwear may catch on fire but there's redemption too. You'll be a victim, a speck, a mote in God's eye but you'll also be a super hero. Your powers? You have two: being able to sit at a lunch counter, elbow to elbow with lumberjacks while wearing spandex bike shorts and an armor plated ass. I know, they aren't the best superpowers but consider the alternative. Your alter ego back at the office is 401K Man. I chose The Divide.

When I dropped out of the icy Absaroka Mountains and onto a dry plateau near Pinedale, Wyoming I felt the tension release. The Divide broke with tradition and offered me a precious gift: a tailwind that pushed me quickly southward. Mile after dusty mile disappeared beneath my wheels while I took shallow breaths and ate fried chicken from a greasy bag on my handlebars. That night I camped on the skin of the Great Basin. From the map I saw that it had been a good day, I'd put more than 130 miles between myself and Sawmill Lodge.

For the first time since Banff the changes in Latitude were obvious, gone were the mud and ice and the horrible rain. They were replaced by grass and blue sky. I saw my first antelope. That night I slept in a soft green meadow cut through by a river with white flowers blooming along the bank. But it wasn't all high fives and ice cream for me on The Divide. I was still injured and the basin loomed ahead.

In the morning I went to the river and filled up my water bottles. Walking on the uneven ground was agony but my bicycle was a sanctuary and I clicked through the gears to Atlantic City, the last stop before things get serious in the basin. The Petervary's had already been through on their mountain tandem and had left the town buzzing. My waitress was talking about them when I arrived, "The lady was nice but that little man... he ate all our candy!" She tut-tutted while taking my order. And then I was gone, headed toward Boo Radley's desert home.

For me, the Great Basin was like poking around a historic battlefield. Tension was in the air, I could sense both catastrophe and triumph but I was just a tourist passing through. I saw in my mind's eye how the featureless hills would bake on a hot day and how the chalky dust could swallow a racer alive. I knew the history of Divide Racing in the basin and felt the tracks from past races rattle my tires. From 2008 I saw Small Block Eights run tightly over by Nanoraptors as Stephen Gleasner desperately chased Siren Mary in cycling's longest ever battle for last place. Below those were the tracks left by Matthew Lee and Mike Curiak, bitter rivals who bickered and dueled their way south in Divide Racing's early years. Of course, Kenny Maldonado's tracks were there, as were Jon Billman's a year later. John Stamstad's mark was easy to spot: chunky and outdated, the tracks from 1999 were arrow straight. Even further back in time, petrified in my imagination, were two tracks left by Mike and Dan Moe who pedaled through the Great Basin in 1984 and helped inspire the GDMBR.

Diagnus Well. Copyright Eric Bruntjen

But that's all I could do; imagine the hardship and drama. In 2009, on the day I raced through the Great Basin as a wounded rider, fragile and vulnerable to any attack, the basin revealed itself to be a creampuff. My tailwind, though lesser than the day before, stayed loyal and the Wyoming sun rose high but feeble. I doubt the temperature ever cracked eighty degrees that day. Even the notorious basin dust stayed glued to the dry ground, allowing me to cruise unimpeded across hill and dale.

Diagnus Well was flowing clear when I arrived. I'd never been to a real desert oasis before and I was disappointed. There were no palm trees, sheiks or nubile young ladies. There was just an old palomino with dopey eyes. It pawed at the ground near some modern approximation of a covered wagon. The horse's owner, a blabbermouth cowboy who'd been annoying the racers ahead of me, was nowhere to be found so I quickly filled up and sped deeper into the basin. I even indulged myself the possibility of visiting an old friend in Rawlins, or at least what was left of him.

Months before, while sitting in front of the computer, my research would sometimes go spectacularly off the rails. Well past midnight I'd find myself pixel blind and half in the bag while wandering around the Rawlins Frontier Museum's online exhibits. That's where I met Big Nose George, a nasty scoundrel who orbited the Great Basin in the late 1800's. He was a cop killer and a bank robber and yes, he had a gigantic nose. In grainy, sepia toned pictures he looks more like a garden tool than an actual human being, like something you could split firewood with.

Like many Divide Racers, Big Nose George met his end on the edge of the Great Basin, though he had it much worse. Caught trying to escape from the Rawlins jail, Big Nose was set upon by a mob of Rawlin's finest and hung dead. Not satisfied with your average frontier lynching the good men and women cut Big Nose down and divvied up his body as souvenirs. Part of his skull ended up as an ashtray while his tanned hide actually made it to an inaugural ball, as a pair of shoes worn by the Governor himself. It's true. You can't make this stuff up.

When I hit Mineral X Road I still held out hope of seeing old Big Nose at the Frontier Museum. The ashtray is there, as are the shoes – under glass and flaccid. In the end it was an impossible thought. The sun was setting and my gas tanks were almost empty. I knew that I wasn't going to make it in time. Besides, Divide Racers don't peruse through museums or anything else on their way to Mexico so I turned my own shoes (cowhide thank you very much) a little faster and raced against the setting sun.

Just south of Rawlins the mountains rise up out of the ground like a wall; your tires actually make a little thump when they hit the vertex of the Rockies. It's an amazing transformation, one that signals to racers that they have survived the Great Basin. I don't remember looking back when I hit that bump the next day but months later I can't get the basin out of my head. It comes back to me in flashes at the strangest times; in a meeting or on the phone. In my mind's eye I can see the oddly blue sage, I hear the antelope crashing through the dry brush and feel the soft basin air that treated me so well but turned wicked on later racers. Boo Radley indeed. The basin waited and watched me race southward but then, at my weakest point, it picked me up. The Great basin may have knocked Kenny Maldonado down and torn Big Nose George apart but it was good to me. It carried me across and set me down on the porch of the Rocky Mountains as a stronger, better racer. There were still challenges ahead - otherworldly rain in Colorado and a peloton of exceptional riders to catch in New Mexico- but my race had turned a corner. Bolstered by success in the Great Basin I reached the finish line at Antelope Wells, New Mexico in twenty one days and twelve hours exactly.

As for Evan Mettie, the paralyzed Iraq War Vet... I raised over $20,000 and we got that all-terrain wheelchair. More than the Great Basin or even the Antelope Wells finish line I remember his Mom's teary, gripping hug.

Divide Haiku

A poem by Ward Grovetch

Spring on The Divide
Dear God I am so hungry
Uh oh Grizzly Bear

Ode to Divide Racers

A poem by Diana C. Gleasner

Listen my friends and you shall hear
A lone mountain bike in the granny gear.
You started in Banff seventeen strong
But this is a tale of things that go wrong

Achilles tendons and drifts of snow,
Grizzlies, big cats, nightmares-to-go.
Miles to go before you sleep
And all those promises to keep.

With lagging spirits and constant grief,
Utter exhaustion with no relief,
Wet, hungry, legs like concrete
Can't feel your toes, can't feel your feet.

Lugging your stuff, not to mention your bike
On this Rocky Mountain obstacle hike.
Some say that it was just never clear
They would need the skills of a mountaineer.

Swarming mosquitoes and one sore butt,
Mud everywhere, your wheels in a rut.
You've climbed 200,000 feet
And endured the desert's relentless heat.

Emotional ups, emotional downs
Mysterious maps, vanishing towns,

Swollen ankles, fever and chills
Slippery paths and a hundred spills

Awesome country these racers have seen -
Canada, Mexico and all parts between
from Banff in Alberta to Antelope Wells.
Each rider enduring their personal hells.

The prize isn't money, nor is it glory
It's just being part of an epic story.
It's you, your bike and your winning smiles.
You made it through nearly 3,000 miles.

It's meeting the challenges, seeing it through
Knowing the one who endured it was you.
Knowing you triumphed on this awesome ride -
Knowing you conquered the Tour Divide.

Reasons to Race

A poem by Leah Hieber

it
is not
like the weeks
when you don't know
what you've done
not the extra work hours for
a forgettable project, not the office potluck and
dress-down Fridays, not watching the news in bed, reminding
yourself to take out the garbage in the morning and get the oil changed
and we're out of milk and I think my computer has a virus
and somebody's birthday is coming if only you
could remember whose.
When every day
looks the
same then
you do it again and
all the resolutions to live each day get lost as if
by corporate design it's not like that it's more like refusing
drugs in order to feel every labor pain so you know that you know the
extent of nature's brutality and that you can survive it.
More like first meeting your great love and
everywhere you went the secret traveled with you
like a bright light shining in your chest so bright that

everyone could see that something wonderful was happening
to you it's more like when you were seventeen and had your first great
heartache but you still kept listening to your song again and again because
it felt good to hurt it's more like your first travels to a country that is truly
foreign, the sudden warm humidity and insects and delirium of
crowds in which all becomes fascination and if you were the
kind of person who prayed you would say that it is
all prayer and it is like when your child first
begins to talk with real words and
you realize that she has been
watching you and
understanding so
much of
what you
say and
thinking
her own
thoughts
and it is like
your first time
walking outside after
the illness you thought
would kill you and thinking
so this is the feeling of air so this
is the scent of sky and although everything
 inside you is nearly broken you have never
known yourself so well as this in this agony and
survival in this sucker-punch from life and you know
that even if things go back to normal they will never be the
same and it is like when you were a kid and you finally managed
to ride without your father's hand on the seat of your bike
and took off all the way down the road and
struggled up the next hill and flew
down again without ever
touching the
brakes.

The Race and the Tour

Scott Morris

My fiancé, Paula Morrison, and I awoke early in the town of Abiquiu, New Mexico. The day before had seen us dodging afternoon hailstorms that turned the Jemez Mountains into a winter wonderland, so we were on the road quickly. We cycled along quiet forest roads that linked small villages with names straight out of Old Mexico: El Rito, Vallecitos and Cañon Plaza. After climbing near the crest of Burned Mountain (10,192 feet), we saw our first mountain biker in 680 miles of cycling the Great Divide Mountain Bike Route (GDMBR). We were riding from Mexico to Canada, but the rider we saw was taking the more traditional North to South route.

It was Mike Curiak, racing in the inaugural Great Divide Race (GDR). He was in first place and intent on breaking John Stamstad's long standing record for the same route. In 1999 Stamstad suffered along the spine of the United States, covering the 2,460 mile off-road route in 18 days and 5 hours. It was an incredible effort, but Curiak was determined to best it.

Curiak was in high spirits, though he was completely out of food and bonking when he met us. GDR racers are allowed to accept help as long as it is not pre-arranged, so he took a Clif Bar, licorice and peanut butter from us. I have never seen anyone so happy to eat a Clif Bar. It was something about the way he unlocked his jaw and ate it as though it were a live fish, tilting his head up and dropping it into his mouth.

He raved about Cisneros Park, a beautiful meadow he had just cycled through, chatting far too long for someone chasing a record, and then sped off down the dirt road in a fury. He was headed to Abiquiu, where, he confessed as though it were a cardinal sin; he was going to get a bit of sleep.

Mike Curiak and Paula Morrison meet on the GDMBR. Copyright Scott Morris.

Sleep is a luxury not afforded to Divide Racers. Today, Curiak estimates he averaged about 4 hours per night. Obviously, this is not the Tour de France, where the clock stops ticking at the end of each stage. On The Divide, each second you spend catching Z's is one the competition can use to gain time.

And the competition was never far behind Mike. As Paula and I set up camp that night along the Rio San Antonio, watching an electric sunset develop before our eyes, a tired Pete Basinger cruised through our camp. Though exhausted he waved and smiled; we cheered him on as best we could. Basinger had spent most of the race chasing Curiak; amazingly he was never more than 5 hours behind!

Paula and I continued riding north the next day with renewed vigor. We endured the rough 4x4 roads of Brazos Ridge, cycled the cool, beautiful Conejos river valley and finally climbed endlessly through alpine meadows to the high point of the route at 11,910 feet (Indiana Pass in Colorado). We followed Curiak and Basinger's tire tracks, which were often deep ruts in the road. One of the most difficult aspects of the GDMBR is dealing with the constant changes in weather. A sudden storm can turn a solid dirt road into an un-rideable, mucky mess. We could see tracks from cycling shoes in the mud, so we knew where the racers had been pushing their bikes.

After dropping a near vertical mile through endless stands of aspen trees, we reached the town of Del Norte, where we could check in on the race. Curiak and Basinger had reached Silver City, New Mexico within 2 hours of each other. With only 125 miles to the finish line at the border of Mexico, it was anyone's race.

As much as we wanted to linger in Del Norte and keep tabs on the race, Paula and I had other priorities; we faced several long climbs to high mountain passes over the next few days and had to get rolling on our own adventure again. In total, the GDMBR climbs some 200,000 feet over its length, which is the equivalent of climbing Mt. Everest seven times from sea level. If you aren't a climber, the GDMBR will quickly turn you into one.

It wasn't until we reached Silverthorne Colorado that we got word about the incredibly close finish of very first Great Divide Race. After falling asleep on the bike at 25 mph, Curiak stopped to take a nap but overslept. Eventually Mike opened his eyes in time to watch Pete Basinger ride by, not ten feet from where he lay.

Curiak packed up his minimal camping gear, chased Basinger down and rode the next 80 miles with him (without drafting, which is not allowed in the race). Curiak had been running scared of Basinger's "strong, determined 23 year-old legs" for most of the race, and now he was facing an all out duel with those legs just 10 miles shy of the Mexican border. Considering the length of the race, it was a sprint finish.

The two cyclists increased their pace during the final 10 miles of desolate Chihuahuan desert, where Curiak's determination and fitness proved too much for Basinger. Mike crossed the Mexican border in a time of 16 days and 57 minutes, his challenger arrived 24 minutes later. Both men had destroyed John Stamstad's record by over two days, but it was Curiak who came out on top.

Curiak's 16 day epic along the Continental Divide may be his most impressive feat ever. On average, he covered 155 miles and climbed over 12,000 feet PER DAY. Most mountain bikers have never done a single day ride of that length. To do sixteen in a row, with no support, is super-human. That's Mike Curiak for you.

Meanwhile, Paula and I were heading north on the Great Divide. Unlike Curiak, we were getting full nights of rest. We carried things like a tent, stove and real food. Only occasionally did we ride at night. We stopped to do hikes off the route and to talk to the locals. But we kept our pace steady, managing to average about 70 miles a day with only two days of rest. We wanted to enjoy the ride, but we also saw it as a great challenge, so we pushed ourselves.

Riding The Divide is an experience. Seeing such incredible scenery, day after day, renewed and refreshed us. There was at least one point during each day where I simply had to stop, stand and stare. It was empowering to ride through such remote country, entirely self sufficient and experience an America that few see.

Our final days of riding through Montana were some of the best. We cycled abandoned roads covered in knee-high flowers, climbed steep mountain passes and saw an abundance of wildlife (no bears, though!). On our final day we met two cyclists at Red Meadow Lake, just beginning the long journey we were about to complete. We smiled at the enthusiasm in their eyes and were jealous of the adventure before them.

We coasted down the final hill into Roosville, Montana as the sunset lit the sky afire. 38 days and 12 hours prior we had stood with the same enthusiasm in our eyes. In the end Paula set a record on the GDMBR that year, but all we could talk about was how incredible the trip had been and how tired we were.

Before the trip I had wondered how Stamstad, Curiak and others could push the limits of the human body throughout their arduous journey. After seeing the landscapes, meeting the people and feeling the air on my face, I felt I understood.

Interview with George Niels Sorensen

Bicycles have a long history on the Continental Divide. Long before John Stamstad completed the first Divide Race, even before Mike and Dan Moe pedaled south to north in the eighties, a group of African American "Buffalo Soldiers" were recruited to showcase the speed and efficiency of bicycles on The Divide. Based out of Fort Missoula the Bicycle Corp made several grueling rides along The Divide before being disbanded. Despite their rudimentary equipment and difficult living conditions the Iron Riders adopted a motto that would be familiar to any modern Divide Racer: Onward.

Portland historian George Niels Sorensen[GNS] wrote a book about the Bicycle Corp titled <u>Iron Riders</u> and recently spent some time with the Cordillera [TC] to discuss pneumatic tires, divide mud and the how easy today's racers have it.

[TC] Could you give us a broad overview of who the Iron Riders were?

[GNS] The Iron Riders, as I've named them in my book, were a group of African American soldiers that rode bicycles at Fort Missoula, Montana in the 1890s. African American Soldiers at that time were usually known as Buffalo Soldiers. The term Buffalo Soldier came from the American Indians who interacted with the black soldiers in what were called the Indian Wars.

After the Indian Wars were over there were a few years during which these soldiers were in Forts, in the American West, without an active battle to fight. That gave James A. Moss, a white Lieutenant, the idea of creating the Bicycle Corps and to try it out with the Buffalo Soldiers stationed at Fort Missoula, Montana. It is interesting to note that Lt. Moss had graduated at the bottom of his West Point class, which gave him this undesirable duty station in Montana. His experiment was an attempt to replace the horse with the bicycle as the Army's mode of transportation.

The Iron Riders in what would become Yellowstone National Park. National Archives photo.

[TC] Could you describe the Iron Rider's bicycles, clothing and kit?

[GNS] The bicycles they used weighed over thirty pounds. They were very heavy and made of iron with rudimentary wheels and rims. ... After adding their equipment the soldiers ended up with bicycles that weighed close to sixty pounds and were very difficult to maneuver

It makes you wonder what today's riders are complaining about when they are riding on titanium frames or bikes that weigh maybe twenty five pounds with suspension as well.

[TC] Divide Racers spend a lot of time keeping their bikes running while out on The Divide. What kind of mechanical problems did the Iron Riders to run into?

[GNS] One of the main problems with the bicycles of that era was that there was no easy way to make a good tire. They tried at first to make solid rubber tires but they were heavy and very hard to ride on. Balloon tires worked but the problem was that you needed an effective valve to keep air in the tire. The problem was the valve itself, they constantly leaked and broke off.

Another problem was attaching the tire to the wheel. The wheels were primitive with ineffective rims to grip the tires. In some cases they tried to glue the tires to the rim and also used other methods of attaching them.

So if a soldier got a flat tire he would have to figure out a way to first repair the puncture and then reattach the tube and tire to the wheel under adverse conditions. Mud would get in there; you had to wipe it off. The glues and patches didn't work very well; temperature and humidity mattered. The entire system was a problem. It must have been very frustrating.

Also, James A Moss [the commanding officer] complained about the vibration that they endured. There was no spring or dampening system on the bike so when they were riding on railroad tracks, to avoid the mud, they would just go kabang, kabang, kabang along the ties. He even suggested adding a spring or a shock to the front tire much like today's mountain bikes routinely have.

[TC] One of the major challenges that Divide Racers face is calorie management, you are out there burning calories like crazy with no way to quickly resupply. Obviously the Iron Riders had it even worse; sometimes their food would run away. Can you tell us how they managed to eat enough food on their longer trips?

[GNS] During the longer trips the Iron Riders would ship supplies ahead to different depots. That was useful because they weren't able to stop at a 7-11 or Safeway. The only other alternative was to trade with farmers along the way. The idea of calorie management wasn't really a concept. They were either hungry or they weren't.

There was a time when the Bicycle Corp organized themselves into a skirmish line and shot at a free roaming chicken. They somehow missed.

One of the ways they managed their exertion was to start early in the morning and ride until the hottest part of the day, say noon, and then take a break. From noon on they wouldn't expend any calories. They'd light a fire, cook a little bacon and then at four o'clock they'd get back on their bikes and ride on into the cooler evening.

Drinking water was also a problem; they'd get sick from the alkaline wells and streams they encountered. Today we don't realize how easy things are compared to how it was over a hundred years ago.

[TC] Divide Racers often complain about five things: cold, heat, rain, mud and more mud. Do you think that would sound familiar to an Iron Rider?

[GNS] The Iron Riders had it worse, they wore wool uniforms, in the summer! They didn't have the luxury of synthetics. They didn't have sunscreen or things like that. If they got hot they took their jacket off, if they got cold they put it on. That just went with the territory.

There was one rider who complained so much that they put him on a train back to Fort Missoula in Montana and he never got to see St. Louis where the training ride ended. That was his punishment.

By comparison today's riders have a pretty easy go of it.

[TC] Divide Racers sometimes have humorous, or not, interactions with locals who live along the route. Did the Iron Riders have any interesting encounters on The Divide?

[GNS] There are stories about small towns being surprised by the Bicycle Corps. People would come out to their porches and just stare. There was an encounter in what would become Yellowstone National Park where they ran into Frederick Remington, the famous Western Artist. He was surprised to see them and wrote about it in Cosmopolitan Magazine.

[TC] The Iron Riders were preparing for a cross-country ride when they were called up to serve in the Spanish-American war. How did that work out for them?

[GNS] This group of Buffalo Soldiers may have been instrumental in saving the life of Teddy Roosevelt who would, of course, go on to become president of the United States. Roosevelt is famous for being a member of the Rough Riders and he has received a lot of notoriety for his work charging up San Juan Hill but the truth is that he was pinned down. He could very well have been killed were it not for a group of Buffalo Soldiers who bailed him out. It may have been the Bicycle Corp soldiers who did that.

[TC] What do you think an Iron Rider would think of Divide Racing? Would they recognize it all?

[GNS] I would like to think that a soldier who served in that period… if he could get on a bicycle that was light weight with tires that didn't leak air and had all this modern equipment and a gps… that he would think he'd just gone to heaven. It would be the most fun thing he could do.

Iron Riders near the Continental Divide, Lieutenant James A. Moss leads. National Archives photo.

Independence Day

Jill Homer

On July 4, I woke up to brilliant sunlight and crisp air. It tasted like morning in the early fall, with hints of seltzer and wood smoke. I stocked up at the last gas station in town and checked my maps for the phone number to the Pie-O-Neer café in Pie Town. I had already accepted that clinging to the hope it would be open on a national holiday was a futile at best, but I had heard entire legends formed around the pie in Pie Town. That one stop was likely my only shot at human interaction in the next 300 miles, so even a futile chance was certainly worth a try. Plus, I would need to restock my drinking water somehow.

At 8:30 a.m., an answering machine informed me that the café was open Wednesday through Saturday, 11 a.m. to 4 p.m. They said nothing about July 4 specifically, but at least there was a chance they were open that day. Still, even my best-case scenario made reaching it seem impossible. Pie Town was 80 miles away. Even if there was no mud on the road, an impossible-sounding prospect in itself, my chances of pedaling that far in just over seven hours were unlikely at best. The answering machine beeped, and without planning to, I suddenly launched into a pleading message.

"Hi, my name is Jill. I'm traveling through town on a bicycle with the Tour Divide. Perhaps you've seen other bikers come through. Anyway, I'm calling from Grants. It's 8:30 a.m. Saturday. I'm going to try to make it there by 4, but it's 80 miles and with the mud, well, it's not very likely I'll be there before you close. I was wondering if you could leave out some kind of lunch, maybe a sandwich or something, and a piece of pie, and a gallon of water, along with a check, and I'll leave cash. I don't even care what it is. I pretty much just need calories at this point, calories and water. Please. I'm good for it. I have a lot of cash. My name is Jill Homer."

Copyright Jill Homer

I set out with determination to make the 4 p.m. deadline, come what may. As the derelict highway buildings of Grants faded behind me, a bubble of emotion expanded inside my gut. I felt a strong mixture of gratitude and love, as well as loneliness, fear and despair. I couldn't discern where all of it was coming from. My situation was positive, even pleasant. I was rested, well-fed and riding on pavement within sight of a town full of people. Despite these comforts, tears started to trickle down my cheeks, which erupted into streams, which erupted into open sobbing, complete with flowing snot and flemmy gulps of air.

Whenever endurance cyclists embark on long races, people often ask us afterward about the specific point when we realized we could finish what we had set out to do. I always dismissed this question as unanswerable and misleading. To some, I would say that I knew I would eventually finish the Tour Divide when I was all the way back in Montana. To others, I admitted that I wasn't even sure when I made the final right turn 65 miles from the border. But if I am truly honest with myself, those minutes I spent sobbing on my way out of Grants stand apart as a defining moment of clarity.

As my tears began to slow and my gasps became softer, I pleaded an open prayer to entities I also felt were indefinable - to God, to my inner strength, to the powers that be. "Please be with me. Please stay with me. Please help me get through this." Something about leaving Grants told me that, barring breakdown or disaster, I was going to finish the Tour Divide. Since I had no control over breakdown or disaster, I pleaded for help from the one thing that might.

The powers that be nodded benevolently and swept me along the smooth corridor of Highway 117. The rugged but sheer cliffs of El Malpais National Monument cast the pavement in cool shadow. After 38 miles, the route joined the washboard ruts of a wide county road. The jittery corduroy soon faded into smooth but soft clay. The area had indeed been pummeled by thunderstorms the night before; blood-colored puddles glistened in the road's many dips and potholes. As I rode, my wheels kicked up large clumps of red mud. Still, beneath the late morning sunlight, the mud had hardened just enough to roll into balls and fling away rather than stick to my bike.

"Think light, be light," I chanted, as though sheer force of will could reduce my weight and keep my wheels floating over the jelly-like layers of mud. Atop a paper-thin veneer of solidified clay, I pedaled apprehensively but quickly, coming close to sinking into the soft mud that undulated beneath my tires, but never quite breaking through the dry layer. I smiled at the knowledge that if I had passed through the same area just a few hours earlier, I would have been mired in wet sludge. Every once in a while, the universe rewards late risers.

Just after 2 p.m., after covering nearly 80 miles in five and a half hours, I strode triumphantly into the open doors of the Pie-O-Neer café. The single-room restaurant was set up modestly with modern tables and old Western art. A guitarist and bassist strummed acoustic country ballads as couples chatted softly over heaping plates of pie. A woman wearing a ruffled apron rushed out from behind the counter and threw her arms around me in a enthusiastic hug. "You made it!" she exclaimed. "I can't believe you made it!"

"I made it," I said, smiling widely.

The guitarist had just finished a cover of Johnny Cash's "Long Black Veil." "So you're Jill?" he asked. I nodded. "We did not think you'd make it here until late tonight," he continued. "It rained all through the night last night, just poured. I knew that road was gone. I sometimes take my horses out there and I know how bad it can get. Even they can't get through the mud sometimes. We thought you'd be stuck in it."

"I thought so, too," I said. "But it had hardened up in the sun. I got really lucky."

"Well, anyway, congratulations on getting here from Grants in just a few hours. That's some incredible riding."

The woman in the apron nodded. "You should have seen Matt Lee when he came through. It was late but I let him in the door. It had been raining. He was covered in mud. He had this crazy look in his eyes and he just fell in the door mumbling, 'I need food.' I said, 'I know you need food but you're not coming in here until you clean off that mud.' I practically had to push him back out the door. I thought, 'This can't be healthy.'"

I laughed. I was about to launch into my "Here in mid-pack, we have more fun" speech when she grabbed my shoulders and rushed me to a nearby table. "But you must be starving, riding all the way from Grants," she said. "What do you want to eat?"

"Um, what do you have?" I asked.

"Well, we don't have much. The menu's over there on the wall."

Before I even looked at it, I asked, "Do you have salad?"

"Well, I don't have salad, but I have some spinach and tomatoes and other veggies in the fridge. Tell you what, I'll make you one."

"That would be awesome," I said.

"And our special today is spinach quesadilla with fresh salsa. We also have a tomato vegetable soup."

"Those sound amazing, too," I interrupted. "I'll have them both. And salad."

"Do you want something to drink?"

"Um …" I wavered. I had already ordered a lot.

"The other Tour Divide guys were just knocking pops back faster than I could replenish them. What do you want?"

"Do you have Pepsi?" I asked.

"Of course," she said.

"And you can't leave here without trying a slice of pie," she said.

"Of course I can't." I took a lingering look at the back wall, lined from end to end with towering desserts. "Um, I'll try the coconut cream," I finally said.

"Good choice," she said. "That one won an award last month from a national magazine."

As I waited for my mountain of fresh food, the guitarist asked me if I had any requests. I couldn't think of many country tunes I even knew, so I requested more Johnny Cash - "Ring of Fire" - and thought about my travels south into the desert regions of the Great Divide as he sang, "I fell in to a burning ring of fire; I fell down, down, down and the flames went higher."

As promised, the woman served up cans of Pepsi faster than I could knock them back, and brought me plate after plate of food, hot and fresh and brimming with all the real nutrition I had scarcely known in three weeks of a diet heavy on junk food from gas stations and greasy spoon diners. The woman asked me how my lunch was. "You have no idea how replenishing it is to eat healthy for a change," I said. "If all Americans could feel this way after eating a spinach salad, McDonalds would go out of business. Which would be awesome, because then people like me could actually find healthy food to eat on the Great Divide."

The woman laughed. She asked me about the trail prior to Grants and I told her about how surprisingly remote New Mexico had been. A man eating pie at the table turned and launched into a stern warning about the dangers of New Mexico's backcountry. "There are cougars out there that hunt people," he said ominously. "I hope you have protection."

I pointed to the can of bear spray I had been carrying since Canada and had never even come close to discharging, unless I counted the time I pointed it at the vicious dogs of Vallecitos. "I'm from Alaska," I said. "So I'm well-versed in the defense against predators thing." I wanted to tell him that I was far more afraid of mud and lightning, of fatigue and bad judgment, of loneliness and fear itself, but it seemed pointless to argue about the most pressing dangers of the Divide.

I spent much longer in Pie Town than I had intended, basking in the warmth of small-town friendliness and scraping up the last remnants of whipped cream from my pie plate. I was so full that I had difficulty breathing normally, but couldn't remember ever feeling more satisfied. I sat back in my wooden chair and listened to the country band croon about an unhurried life I had all but forgotten.

In the late afternoon, the woman in the apron and guys in the band walked outside to see me off. "It's just about closing time and we're all headed to the lake," she said. "But you have a great ride, and don't hesitate to come back when you're through these parts again. Happy Independence Day!"

"You too," I said, shaking all of their hands. "Thanks for making the best lunch in the entire span of the Rocky Mountains."

I left Pie Town at 4 p.m. into a brand new day. I felt like I was just waking up from a restful sleep, even though I had 80 miles behind me. "Someday," I thought, "I'm going to be a veteran of this race and people will ask me the secret to success. I'm going to answer, 'human kindness.'"

The roller coaster terrain made two nondescript crossings of the Continental Divide. I pedaled past ranches and cut into a canyon, surrounded again by large, triangle-shaped mountains. The remote road intersected with an abandoned town site, an old Spanish mission. I got off my bike and explored the eerie remnants of a slab and mortar church, peering into the cracks of boarded windows and gazing up at a hollow bell tower.

Just beyond the town site, I entered Gila National Forest. My maps informed me: "Camping OK next 14 miles." I pedaled beneath gnarled and grand juniper trees, rising back into the ponderosa forest, and cresting the Continental Divide once again at a spectacular overlook of the San Agustin plains below. I could see thunderstorms building over the distant mountains beyond the valley. It was still early in the evening. "If I don't stop near here," I thought, "I'll have to pedal all the way through that valley before I'm back in a spot where I can camp." But I was feeling too incredible to stop. I launched into a gleeful descent toward the darkening sky.

The Forest Service road bisected a remote state highway and crossed onto a country road sparsely lined with private ranches. An occasional ranch house broke the monotony of the sagebrush plains, but for the most part I was wholly alone in sweepingly open space. The wind blew briskly at my side, whipping around and changing directions intermittently as booms of thunder clattered across the desert.

The thunderstorm I had seen hanging over the horizon began to close in. The bulk of the storm seemed to be moving the same direction I was, but I was approaching it faster than it was streaming away. I glanced over my shoulder and noticed another storm approaching from behind. Sheets of pouring rain hung like curtains beneath black clouds, and frequent flashes of lightning broke through the darkness.

A primal sense of entrapment gripped my core. My heart pounded. I was pedaling in a tiny window of calm, chasing one violent storm even as another chased me. If I pedaled too fast, I would catch the first storm. If I pedaled too slow, I would be caught by the second storm. I shivered at the prospect of both scenarios, and vowed to do everything in my cycling power to hover in the hurricanes' eye.

It was shortly after I made this decision that I heard a sickeningly loud zipping sound shoot out from the back of my bike. The rear tire became more and more bouncy and sluggish until I had no choice but to stop and deal with the flat. I had been using "Slime" inner tubes, which were filled with green sealant intended to coat and block any holes that happened to be punctured in the tube. They had worked beautifully for the duration of the Divide, and I had yet to spring a leak that wasn't quickly blocked, requiring only a few refresher hits from my air pump. This was the first time a tire had gone completely flat. It was my rear tire, which required the loosening of the brake caliper before I could remove the wheel. A rear flat change usually took me at least 10 minutes when I was fresh, and as many as 20 when I was hurried and frustrated. I knew I did not have 20 minutes to spare before I would be caught directly beneath a barrage of lightning and rain. I did not even have 5 minutes.

"Be brave," I chanted through gulping breaths as I hopped off the bike. "Be strong."

A thick streak of green slime coated the down tube of the frame. I was sure all the sealant had leaked out and there was nothing left to fill the hole. But it was possible that I had just sprung a larger leak that took a while to clog. It seemed worth a try to pump up the tire rather than change the tube right away. The extra time it would take if it didn't work wasn't going to save me from the storm either way, but if that's all it took, there was still a chance I could outrun the air strike.

I breathed in and out with every stroke of the air pump, continuing to chant, "Be brave. Be strong." As I pumped, the sun slipped beneath the nearest mountains. The sky, already under siege, burst open in an explosion of crimson and gold light. The sudden blast of color reflected off the dark clouds in a contrast so bright that the entire sky shimmered. Where sunset's saturated light met the sheets of rain, broad rainbows swept over the desert. I counted five rainbows at one point, arched in wide spans that framed the phosphorescent clouds. And beneath the rainbow stage, steaks of lightning performed a violent ballet.

The scene did nothing to reduce the panic gurgling in my gut. But from where I sat in my shrinking window of peace, trying my best to breathe to the rhythm of my air pump, I knew that I was witnessing a moment of powerful beauty - beauty that was more powerful even than fear. I briefly closed my eyes and tried to absorb the awe, the sheer terror and wonder that nature was unleashing before me. I felt like I was clinging to the precipice between heaven and hell, and if I happened to fall, no matter which direction I went, I would be wholly absorbed forever.

I snapped my eyes back open and injected a few last shots of air into the tire. It was still fairly soft, about 20 psi, but I didn't hear any more of that terrible zipping sound, and I thought there was a better than even chance that it would hold the air. I hopped back on the saddle and pedaled wildly, trying to regain the distance I had lost on the second storm. I pedaled right into the heart of the largest, brightest rainbow and its undulating electric dangers. I was still fully aware that I was the tallest object for miles, on an open plain without even a sagebrush bush large enough to huddle behind. I briefly thought about veering off on a ranch road and sprinting one or two miles to the nearest structure in search of shelter, but I fought the urge. "Be brave," I chanted. "Be strong."

The spectacular light of the sunset lingered much longer than I even thought possible, as though it, like me, was afraid to fade into the darker regions of eternity. It didn't take long to catch the aftermath of the first storm. The road was coated in wet mud and two-inch-deep puddles, but the sky overhead remained mercifully dry. The second storm slowed its advance and started to move mercifully to the east. As it changed its course, the front storm followed. My own route veered west and began climbing back into the mountains.

When I reached the mouth of a canyon, I stopped one last time to look out over the plains of San Agustin. Sunset's crimson and orange flames were almost snuffed out, except for thin, blood-colored streaks that still bordered the horizon. Lightning continued to pierce the purple twilight, followed closely by booms of thunder. As I watched the storm march east, I noticed tiny blue flashes of light erupting from the northern horizon. They confused me at first - they were too low to be lightning, but too large and sporadic to be light from a ranch house. I squinted and realized they were fireworks, set off over a ranch at least 20 miles distant.

"Oh yeah," I said out loud. "It's the Fourth of July." I turned my focus to the fireworks, watching the tiny streams of blue light sparkle and then fade, over and over, as flashes and booms of lightning and thunder nearly overwhelmed the tiny celebration.

"Why don't they just look up and realize that the most spectacular show is going on in nature?" I wondered. Their efforts seemed so small and pathetic in a world that was so vast and so powerful. Humans were nothing out here, nothing at all.

Darkness encompassed me with the rising canyon. For a while I could still hear the thunder, and then only the wind and stillness. Rainwater coated the road and the air was moist and cool. The last tailing clouds of the storms were starting to break apart. A nearly full moon rose overhead, casting a ghostly glow on an assemblage of sandstone hoodoos that bent like petrified zombies in front of craggy cliffs. I rolled out my sleeping bag on the bare dirt beneath the a cluster of ponderosa pines. Moonlight filtered through a canopy of needles. With what felt like a paltry sprinkling of effort and a heavy dose of grace, I had knocked out 140 miles in the 14 hours behind me, with only 250 more to go.

"Thank you," I said in continuation of my morning prayer. "That was a good day."

Divide Racing from Where I Sit

Joe Polk

I will speak of racing the Great Divide Mountain Bike Route as a whole. Since the now larger Tour Divide was born of the original Great Divide Race, the two are inexorably tied from the womb of the route, as it were.

It was my fascination with written updates from the Great Divide Race that led me to pursue adding audio call-ins to my webcast, MTBCast, for 2006 and beyond. My conversations with Mike Curiak at the time were mostly trying to explain why anyone would want to hear the often muffled, static-laced calls from racers in far-flung Wyoming cow towns. In the end, I was successful and thus provided a way for racers to be heard by both fans and family via the Internet. Today, we can hear for ourselves the stories and voices from both races!

To me, it's the stories from the trail that make the race. There are so many moments over the past four years that stand out. In 2006, I remember Dave Nice having his fixie stolen as he slept road-side in Montana. Bummed and dejected, he headed home to Denver where his buddy Scott Taylor of Salvagetti Bikes was already setting up a fund to replace Dave's only means of transportation. I believe that was also the first year we got a glimpse of John Nobile's fairing setup, which in 2008 would help him set a new record. Who can forget Kent Peterson setting the original Single Speed record in 2005? And Jeff Kirby finding oddities along the trail: first it was a starry-eyed, albeit drunken, couple who fell in love with him and then in 2009 it was Josh the Lizard Man who would nearly spook Jeff out of the race!

I believe in 2008 it was Artie Olson relaying a story of riding across the basin in the fog, flanked, just barely in sight, by running Mustangs. Jay and Tracey Petervary then finished the Tour Divide route on a tandem in 2009 and, to the surprise of many, finished third overall. There are many more stories that we can only get traces of; from the choked-up rider who has to pull from the race to the nearly anonymous late finisher who still feels like a super hero at Antelope Wells. Everyone takes something from The Divide.

Over the past four years many things have changed, of course. We now have two races, the Great Divide Race and the Tour Divide. Both share a common spirit. In many ways, they take the Tour de France and turn it on its head. They replace ribbons of smooth asphalt with rugged trail and Jeep roads. Sag wagons become stops at small stores, out of the way restaurants, or a simple creek-side snack from the bottom of a bike pack. There are no teams, but rather you may find yourself crossing Wyoming's Great Basin alone, hoping you have enough water on board to get you across.

And when you finally manage to reach the end of the race, there is no podium, only a phone call and a final message to record. One thing remains the same for all, the satisfaction of finishing!

Perspective

John Stamstad

Editor's Note: John Stamstad is a member of the Mountain Bike Hall of Fame and the first person to ever race The Divide. In 1999 John completed what was then the entire route in 18 days and 5 hours, an incredible achievement at the time. The driving principle behind both of today's group start races (the Tour Divide and Great Divide Race) is to recreate not only John's individual time trial but also the spirit of his unsupported adventure.

When I first heard about the plan of the Great Divide Mountain Bike Route, there was never even a question that I would do it. I *had* to do it. I started mountain biking way back in the early 80's when my only objective was to ride the hardest routes in the world. It was my only reason for existing and everything I did and thought about revolved around that one goal for a more than a decade.

Back then I didn't know why I was consumed with extreme challenges, only that I had to do it and that I loved every single second of it. With GDMBR I couldn't imagine anything harder than riding nonstop for 2500 miles on dirt. It was a revelation but I didn't know exactly why.

Growing older, I realized that the beauty of the GDMBR, or any long trail for that matter, has nothing to do with the route, has nothing to with your bike, your gear, your food. Rather, it is an opportunity to look at your soul, to give you a totally unique perspective into what matters in your world. This can be a good or bad thing… depending on perspective.

And that is a lesson that sometimes that takes a few repetitions to sink in.

Despite my passion for long trails, I spent my career as a pro bike racer doing 24 hour races. Riding in circles faster than the next guy was not my passion, it was my profession. I did those races for a living in order to be able to do things like The Divide which I did for *me*.

If you were to ask me why I am on this earth, my answer would be to run/bike/whatever -the mode doesn't matter- the longest and hardest routes in the world. I am good at it not because I have a high vo2max but because I crave it. I need the bleeding edge.

Take, for example, the Iditasport race in Alaska (I've forgotten the year): I was going over Rainy Pass, it was insanely cold, the wind was screaming, it was a complete whiteout, the trail was impossible to find. There was no one to help me, no one to look for me; it was the most alone I have ever felt. Live or die, it was up to me. There was no one else to blame.

John Stamstad in 2009. Copyright Aaron Teasdale

Cordillera

It took every single element of my soul to get through that, I had to be perfect; I had to concentrate like never before. It is times like that, where I am operating at 100% capacity as a human, surviving in the elements, when I get energized. That is when I feel most alive. My eternal quest is to always get back to that place.

My advice to those racing the GDMBR today is to focus on the journey, not the goal. It doesn't matter how fast you do it, no one cares. What matters are the stories you will tell and what you learn about yourself.

I have learned many lessons, many times, but for me the best example is one I learned from an Old Woman on a John Muir Trail run:

While laying down on a rock in the sun to warm up for a bit I looked up and saw a very tan, beautiful, gray haired woman looking at me. She seemed incredibly comfortable with herself as she sat down next to me and looked at all my gear. She said, 'Looks like you have some decisions to make.' I said yes, I am trying to finish this trail but I just don't know if I can do it, I have only slept 3 hours in 4 days, my feet are totally destroyed, my shoes are falling apart, my back is a mess and I am almost out of food.

She seemed almost boringly unconcerned with my excuses and replied, "Why are you here?" I went into a long explanation of how I was running the 225 mile trail, unsupported, while trying to set a speed record. But I was failing. She gave me an all-knowing smile and looked at me with old-soul penetrating eyes and said: "But, why are you *here?*" And then she just got up and walked away...

I opened my eyes, and tried to figure out what had just happened. "Why are you here?" Did I fall asleep? It felt too real to be a dream. I looked all over the ground to find someone's tracks, none. I ran up the trail to see if anyone was there. Nothing. It seemed too real to be a dream. I have never been so affected by something like that. I never even *have* dreams but the whole run was starting to feel like one big feverish vision.

Later, I started to think about it, what did she mean 'why am I here?'... But then the obvious dawned on my sleep deprived brain. She wasn't asking about the details of my run, she wanted to know *why* I do these sorts of adventures.

In the end I didn't finish the JMT, I failed. I quit. But I also succeeded by realizing that I don't do adventures to set records; I don't do them to check trails off my list. I do it for the journey, the personal growth, the experience. I do it to have the old woman visit me and remind me of what is important. I can't get that driving my minivan in suburbia. I can't get it riding in circles faster than the next guy. I get it on the long trail.

For me in '99 the GDMBR worked through a major personal life issue, I was going through a divorce and the individual race gave me the time and perspective to work through all of the issues that surrounded it. Having the time to ride the GDMBR, and life experiences that came from it are valuable to me. I didn't make much money racing a bicycle for a living but those experiences have made me a wealthy man.

So I ask, you: when you are 80 do want to tell your grandkids that you made company X lots of money or do you want to tell them about an Old Woman who visited you in a dream when you lose your perspective?

And the Winner is...

Paul Howard

Once upon a time, there was a bicycle race that wanted to be the toughest, most demanding bicycle race in the whole world. The physical and logistical challenges involved in the inaugural event demonstrated the scope of its ambitions. Participants would be required to cover a scarcely imaginable distance over terrain once considered inaccessible to cyclists. Sleep deprivation, uncertain availability of supplies and appalling road conditions were all to be taken for granted. There were even bears in the more remote sections of the course. Finishing would be a success in its own right. More than just a sporting challenge, however, the new race had the potential to become an icon of the region and culture that had inspired it. Accordingly, the route was designed to exploit the natural beauty of the country in which it was set. It was also intended to draw together a land of widely disparate regions where skepticism of the centre was a mainstay of political thought. In time, it was hoped, the event would become a beacon of national and sporting prestige. For the moment though, it was just a bicycle race, and that bicycle race was the Tour de France.

Sound familiar? Unlikely as it now seems, the origins of the Tour de France and the Tour Divide – indeed Divide Racing in general – have more in common than might at first be imagined. For a start, it's no exaggeration to say that most French roads in 1903 were in a state not unlike that of their current North American Forest Road counterparts. It might have been called a road race – indeed the invention of the mountain bike was still 70 years away– but it bore scant resemblance to the high tech, light weight world of road racing as we know it today. And while it's fair to say that, even over a century ago, there were very few bears left in France and that the Tour de France itself didn't venture into their last mountain strongholds until several years later, the perception of risk and remoteness persisted. As recently as 1947, during the first Tour after the Second World War, French rider Apo Lazaridès was reputed to have stopped, when in the lead on Col d'Izoard, for fear of riding into bear country on his own; clearly he wasn't cut out for cycling in the Rockies.

What's more, although the Tour de France has always been divided into stages, the length of these stages in the Tour's early years, combined with the poor quality of the roads and bikes used meant endurance and resistance to sleep deprivation was as essential then as it is in the Tour Divide today. The longest ever Tour de France stage, repeated regularly until the 1930's, was 482km (over 300 miles) from Les Sables d'Olonne in the Vendée to Bayonne, almost reaching the Spanish border. The average stage length of the longest ever Tour de France (in 1926) was 338km (211 miles). Then there's the intriguing, compelling and oft-repeated attitude of the Tour's martinet founder, Henri Desgrange. No stranger to physical endeavor – he had been one of the earliest holders of the hour record on a bike and ran for two hours every day until well into his seventies – he declared that the perfect race would be one in which only one rider finished. In which case Divide racing has already achieved in less than a decade, the still-unfulfilled goal Desgrange set for the Tour de France over a century ago.

Nowadays, of course, the differences between the two races are far greater than their historical similarities, and it doesn't take a compendious knowledge of either event to be aware of the most obvious distinctions. Lance Armstrong and his colleagues may have to confront physical and sporting battles on an epic scale during their three week odyssey around France, but it's unlikely that any of these challenges involve wrestling with bears. Although, having said that, in 2003, I rode the route of the Tour de France on the day of the race itself, and very early one morning, during a stage in the Pyrenees, I became convinced that I had seen a bear in the flesh (at least until I awoke from the hallucinatory stupor that pre-riding the Tour de France can induce on unprepared journalists). Additionally, Lance et al are unlikely to experience some of the considerable benefits that complement the risks of

Divide Racing. I defy even the most focused athlete to have the true appreciation of solitude that time on your own in the boundless forests of northern Montana can generate. After five days of solo riding from Eureka to Butte last year, punctuated only by brief encounters with local residents, it is little exaggeration to say that I knew more about my psychological make-up than I had ever considered possible (and maybe desirable), even if I felt at times on the verge of losing my sanity.

Then there's the other side of the coin – the companionship experienced both with other riders and those met in passing along the route. I'm sure there's great camaraderie on the Tour de France, but the sheer scale of the event – nearly 200 riders and ten times as many hangers on – makes for an, at times, alienating experience even amongst the participants. Certainly, in 2003, when I rode ahead of the Tour de France, there were times when I felt alienated not just from the vastness of the event itself but also from the country through which I was cycling. To have such an experience while on a bicycle, that most intimate form of transport, was an unexpected and not entirely pleasant revelation. Delightful villages and stunning scenery were certainly encountered, but the logistical challenge of a route that wasn't contiguous required a succession of transfers between soulless chain hotels in out-of-town commercial estates. (Actually, there were a few of those on the Tour Divide too.) In the Tour Divide, at least at the rear of the field where I mainly languished, the sense of shared endeavor and mutual – psychological – support was heightened by the strict insistence on self-reliance. Our struggles were our own, but we were all in it together. As a result, I made friends for life, even if sometimes on the basis of the most fleeting of encounters.

And who could not enjoy the wealth of unlikely experiences each ride seems to inspire? Even the earliest Tour de France racers, with their café raids for food and bottles of wine (even champagne) could not comprehend sharing coffee and whiskey with a cowboy in the middle of a desert or singing karaoke with local ranchers in Sargents, still giddy with joie de vivre at having survived an apocalyptic thunderstorm on Marshall Pass; or… the list is almost endless.

This intimacy with the people who make up the invariably proud, frequently isolated, often beautiful, sometimes mournful communities encountered on the Tour Divide route also provides a unique insight into the geographical and cultural significance of the Rockies in the development of America. It is now possible for even an interloper from overseas such as myself to see how the Tour Divide can aspire to create its own niche in the rich iconography of the Wild West.

Perhaps the most important distinction between the Tour de France and the Tour Divide comes from an underlying raison d'être. Right from its conception, the Tour de France was designed as a means to generate publicity and sell newspapers. That's not to say that the sporting element of the plan was entirely contrived to fuel Desgrange's innate megalomania, but the immediate catalyst for the creation of the Tour de France was as a riposte from one newspaper editor to another in a bitter circulation and advertising battle. Clearly, as the ongoing pre-eminence of the Tour de France demonstrates, Desgrange emerged victorious. Yet this success has been tempered over the years by changes to the race brought about by relentless commercialization. Desgrange's desire for a challenge so difficult that all but the victor would fall by the wayside has been overwhelmed by the process of creating a global sporting spectacle in which only the elite participate. There is today no opportunity for amateurs nor even the semi-pro touriste-routiers of the early days to take part. There is also no motive to see attrition rates at such a level that the favorites cannot finish; as hard as it is, the difficulties cannot be overwhelming or the spectacle – and the revenues for all involved – would diminish.

Perversely enough, the as yet unmitigated difficulties of Divide Racing have so far ensured that it remains much more inclusive. The only limits to participation are personal. More importantly, so are the rewards for participating. There is no fame and fortune associated with riding or even winning the Tour Divide (well, a degree of fame, perhaps, for the winners). It really is the taking part that counts. The Tour de France may be Olympian in scale and intensity, but it is the Tour Divide that is Olympian in philosophy. Long may it remain so.

Divide Racing Bingo

 **A Feeling of Insignificance**	 **Food Poisoning**	 **Pie Town**
 **Biblical Rainstorms**	 **Antelope Wells**	 **Vallecitos N.M**
 **Grizzly Bear**	 **GDMBR Touring Cyclist**	 **Broken Bike or Body Part**

Epic Evolution

Tony Huston

"In the long run, men hit only what they aim at. Therefore, they had better aim at something high."
-Henry David Thoreau

On a humid summer day, thirty five thousand feet above the simmering Texas landscape, I looked up slowly from my August 2008 issue of Outside Magazine and stared, awestruck, into the face of Destiny.

That was the name of the stewardess who was attempting to issue me a bag of Southwest Airlines brand peanuts. Destiny. I wasn't particularly seeing *her*, though, for a magical vision was brewing rapidly in my mind's eye...a dream of glorious adventure and ultimate individualism. Seductive visions of sun kissed mountaintops and rolling seas of alpine canopies danced in my head, with me, The Star, in the midst of it all. Biking alone on a forgotten country road, my reflection speeding along the surface of a glittering blue lake. There was no life-sapping tedium in that dream...no bills to pay, no job to worry about, no obligations to fulfill. There was only the euphoric singing of my soul as I willed myself towards greatness, one pedal stroke at a time.

SLAP! The sting of Destiny's palm on my cheek told me I'd been unknowingly drooling at her face and muttering something about "conquering a divide." Worse, she took back the peanuts. I like peanuts.

I jest about poor Destiny, but the rest is true. Along with a horde of other romanticists and vagabonds-at-heart, I learned about the Great Divide Race and, subsequently, the Tour Divide from Jon Billman's article "The World's Toughest Bike Race is Not in France," and I was spellbound. "People DO this?" I repeatedly asked an invisible Jon Billman while pointing at my magazine quizzically. For every word was a siren song to my city-worn ears. Here was an unimaginable event that took everything I loved...biking, hiking, camping, eating like crap all day long...and rolled it all into a herculean race through the most gorgeous mountain chain I'd ever visited. (Yes, it's the *only* mountain chain I'd ever visited). As I read and re-read that fateful article, it became less of another man's account and more of a direct challenge to me. Gazing at pictures of divide racing greats like Jay Petervary and Matthew Lee riding into the wilds on their super keewwl kitted out bikes, I knew I was going to accept that challenge. I was going to race The Divide. It wasn't a decision. It just *was*.

Mind you, I didn't say I was going to *excel* at racing The Divide. I'd never raced anything in my life, unless you count the time that my unsecured Trek was nudged loose from the tree it was leaning on, and I, subsequently, raced it down a ridge on foot, trying to intercept it before it drowned itself in the stream at the bottom. I lost that race, but I have no fear of losing in the Tour Divide. For this is an adventure with no podium or material prizes awaiting any finisher. The kind of person that answers such a challenge probably considers material prizes meaningless anyway. In my mind, if you can get yourself and your rig to the starting line on race day and begin pedaling south, you've already won.

With the sketchy idea that I was going to compete in 2010, I came home after that trip and dove right into training. The problem, of course, was that I had no idea how to train. I was 35 at the time, with only a few sporadic stints as a weekend warrior under my belt, and those stints were cast aside and forgotten long, long ago. They may as well have been a stack of Britney Spears CD's. I'd also been growing a lovely bacon jacket for years, which, in a stunning testament to the human capacity for denial, I'd been calling muscle. ("Wow, I look even 'stronger' today than I did last week!") Throw in the fact that I lived in southeast Houston, whose humid, smoggy flatlands were not exactly ideal training grounds for a race in the mountains, and that I had no gear, maintenance skills, navigational acumen, money, time or a decent bike, and...wait...why in the hell am I doing this again?

Yes, the myriad of personal obstacles in my way was vast indeed, but I was too stubborn to heed them. I plowed forward bull headedly. I researched, I obsessed, I trained, I bought gear, I got married, I stopped buying gear, I stopped training, I sold my bike, and I got drapes. Kidding, of course. My wife has been wonderfully supportive of my quest, and I love her all the more for it, but hey, I went 35 years without being able to make married jokes. I'll spend the rest of my life milking them for all they're worth. The point is that in the last year and a half I've been busting my hump like at no other time in my life, trying to transform myself from gooey ultranoob into some semblance of an endurance rider. I cannot tell you how I wound up with the aforementioned hump, I only know I've been busting the hell out of it, and my road to Banff has been long and arduous in so many more ways than I care to detail here, since the reader will have their fill of grand tales of suffering and swollen testicles in other parts of this book.

Instead, I would like to present an account of my motivations, experiences and rewards, which I've already gleaned from this journey even though I've not raced a single mile yet. Now, I know what you're thinking. You're thinking, "I bet his story has nothing to do with the Michelin Man, Darth Vader and a porky Oompa Loompa." Well, you're wrong.

There are a hundred reasons why a person may choose to undertake the challenge of the Tour Divide. Like many riders, I view this race as an opportunity to accomplish something great in my life, something absolutely epic, which only a relative handful of people worldwide would ever attempt. It is the chance for me to break away from the tedium of society as usual and forge my own grand tale of adversity and triumph in the unspoiled wilds, to be forever held dear in my heart. Beyond that, however, I want to really get inside my own head with a bright flashlight. The long hours of exertion, discomfort, loneliness, and suffering inherent in a race of this scale has an enormous effect on the psyche, I am told. Veteran riders say that the TD can change a person forever. It's a mysterious promise. What will I find out about myself out there? What epiphany might I have about my being, about life? If I pull into a gas station bathroom in New Mexico, over 2000 miles removed from my life before the Tour, who will I see looking back at me in the mirror? Most importantly, will I have confronted my failings? My fears? Will I handle it like Luke Skywalker did when he entered the dark cave on Dagobah and was confronted by Darth Vader, who he didn't know was really his dad at the time, but also, really, it was himself dressed like his dad, so he dutifully chopped off his own head without knowing that it was his own head and also his dad's head, and when the head stopped rolling around on the ground, it revealed Luke's own face inside the mask staring up at him all creepy like? Yeah…I'm definitely looking forward to that the most.

Cordillera

Without a doubt, the gifts that the Tour Divide may one day give me, be they for better or for worse, will make for the overall grandest and richest adventure of my life. In fact, throughout my year and a half of training and transformation, I have already gained a wealth of experiences and rewards. I recall with great fondness the first time I encountered the dreaded BONK. It was early in my self-concocted training regime, when my rides of mind-boggling distances such as 10 miles, 12 miles and 14 miles required little in the way of refueling. I was just happy to gradually increase my saddle time. That is until the day I did 14 miles and then decided to immediately do the same route again, doubling my best output to date. No food, no energy gel, nothing. Smooth move, that.

Somewhere along the way, the wall came crashing down, and I entered the Twilight Zone. As I continued to slowly crank the pedals through my vibrant new world, drooling and sagging all over my bike frame, I was a tad bit horrified when I looked into the woods and saw a vision of the Michelin Man flitting about in the trees. He was amazingly agile for his size, and he easily kept pace with me, stopping once in awhile to peek coyly at me from behind a gnarled branch. "Screw you, Michelin Man! Come out and face me!" I wanted to scream, but I could only manage a defiant whimper. I knew I would not make it back home, so I tried to board a Greyhound bus back to Deer Park, where I lived. The driver told me that it was impossible to take me to Deer Park because I was already in Deer Park. Also, this wasn't actually a bus but a JC Penny's women's department. And also the driver wasn't a driver but a make-up counter trainee. Realizing my faux pas, I tried to save face by asking her what type of eye liner would match my flesh tone. Kidding about that last bit, but the Michelin Man certainly did toy with me, and, as lame as this may sound to some, I treasure that experience. It is now my story to tell.

Mind you, I made damn sure that I would never bonk again. As my distances increased, I began learning about fuel and performance. I began to fine tune the type and quantity of food I ate during rides. One type of fuel I have recently done away with is energy gel, those packets of thick, slimy, fruity yuckishness found in every bike shop in America. Every time I choked one down I could not help but imagine that I was swallowing the mating juice of a chubby, orange haired Oompa Loompa engaged in his own mischievous packaging process at the factory. Now that I've been doing multi-day rides of 100 miles, I have thankfully ejected those paltry 100 calorie packets from my life and have begun eating the Food of the Gods; M&M's, Skittles, Fritos, chocolate milk, Pop Tarts....I shove it all down my word-hole while getting fitter and losing weight, too. Oh yeah, baby, I am livin' the dream!

In my never-ending quest to find more challenging training grounds than flat old Houston, I have traveled to beautiful new places all over Texas that I would have never visited otherwise and met new people I'd have never otherwise known. Their faces and their stories become chapters in my quest. My favorite encounters was on a long, peaceful road near Somerville Lake, where I met a grizzled older fellow riding a contraption that he'd brought forward through time with him, or at least that's what I reckoned upon first site. It was a vintage bicycle that he had restored, and he claimed he'd been riding it across the country for many years now. As I pressed him for details about how his adventure came to be, he produced an ancient photograph and said, "Here is a picture of me and my bike when I was younger," to which I replied, "*Every* picture of you is from when you were younger!" "True", he said, and explained that he was traveling east to west on the Southern Tier bicycle route, mapped by the Adventure Cycling Association. We were standing on the route, and I hadn't even known it. He told me a little bit of his saga...his family was gone, he'd never traveled much before he began riding, and this life had healed him. He was very wizened and road savvy and, when he found out what I was training for, I sensed he held back a response of "that's cute" and instead gave me some meaningful advice. He had no blog, no email address, he didn't even have a computer on his bike. After twenty minutes or so, he bade me farewell and good luck, and he pedaled his contrivance down the road. That was the last I ever saw or heard from him, and some part of me feels richer for having met him.

Physically, I have attained a level of fitness that had previously been reserved only for actors playing Spartans in the movie "300." Well, ok, I'm still not THAT awesome, but I've come a long way and may yet be invited to dine in Hell by the time it's all said and done. When I first began training, I would feel devastated after coming back from a ride of 25 miles or more, and it would take me several days to feel "normal" again. I seriously questioned my ability to ever get fit enough to attempt a multi-day ride, let alone the Tour Divide. The "q" word popped around in my head more than once, and I came very close to eschewing my saddle for the nestling warmth of my couch indention, where I would continue growing my natural base layer in comfort. Until, that is, I pulled myself aside and had a little talk with myself. "Alright us, listen up. I don't like you, and you don't like me. Obviously we both agree that we are somehow still massively sexy, but people who sip lard through straws and watch American Idol all night never accomplish anything, so get up, shut up, learn to love the pain and RIDE!" I did just that and, as the weeks and months went by, so grew my "Big List of Firsts." My first 30 mile ride, my first 40 mile ride, my first 70 mile ride, my first overnighter, my first race and, most recently, my first 100 mile multi-day with full TD kit. Each and every new "first" is an absolute thrill. The sense of accomplishment, the increased fitness, the dwindling of the meat skirt....these are all the wonderful byproducts of training for my epic saga. When I see folks sneaking peeks at my shapely man-hips, I give thanks to the Tour Divide for the motivation it has given me.

Of course, I might be remiss if I didn't mention the terrible dark side of training for the Tour Divide. Oh, you didn't know? Yes, indeed, there is a terrible and compulsory event that I have suffered through and continue to suffer through, as I am sure every divide racing hopeful must also endure to some degree in trying to haul themselves to Banff. Some may call it "life's many obstacles," others may call it "part and parcel" to divide racing. I call it...The Unshackling!

As I have learned, The Unshackling is the unique process of orchestrating a monumental confluence of events in your life that must harmoniously mesh before June in order to allow you to go and screw off in the wilds for an entire month. The bigger your family, the more abundant your possessions, the more reliant your job is on you, and the more involved your role in society is, the greater your Unshackling process will be. You must, in a fashion, find your own way into becoming Alexander Supertramp on two wheels.

Life will fight you, friend! When it gets word of what you're doing, Life will hurl as many rods in your cogs as it can in order to derail you. Is "rods in your cogs" even a real thing? I don't know, but I certainly feel as if my cogs have been rodded repeatedly and violently at times during my quest. And if you think I'm kidding, then perhaps you've never experienced the pleasure of having the collective dookie of your entire neighborhood enter your home through your shower drain the night before you were supposed to buy your new 29er? Yep, that happened to me and my family as I struggled to make my dream happen. It was a horrifying chapter in my young marriage, and it effectively brought my progression to an abrupt halt. Somehow, we made it through only to immediately begin doing battle with a further plethora of pleasantries. I cannot even speak of one event that threatened to end my bid, as I may well incriminate myself!

And alas, two of my friends, including my faithful training buddy Pat Smith, have fallen victim to The Unshackling's wicked machinations and have had to abandon their goals of racing the TD with me. They are not alone.

I have heard veterans say that The Unshackling (although they don't actually call it that) is much tougher to overcome than the race itself. It is a different process for all of us with varying degrees of difficulty, but even it can be of value. It necessitates mental toughness, perseverance and craftiness, all traits needed to race the TD, or so I would assume. Rising to the unique challenges that it presents has taught me many memorable lessons. Lessons about how to scoop other peoples crap out of my home, I suppose.

As I write this, the 2010 Tour Divide is only three and a half months away and, although I am still dealing with uncertainty due to my own Unshackling process, I am pushing forward, full steam ahead. I've put a great deal of myself into this thing, sacrificing and risking so very much in the process, but living my life in pursuit of such a marvelous goal has been an endless source of self-affirmation. It has truly given me a sense of focus and rediscovered vitality. Honestly, I feel as if some dormant beast has been awakened in me, and it must be fed. A plate full of 2,745 miles shall be its dinner. If, perchance, the stars do not align for me this year, then I will set my site on next year, and I will continue to revel in the copious rewards that have been bestowed on me during this journey.

Lastly, I daresay that no man or woman makes it to Banff purely under their own gumption. The Tour Divide may be a race of individuals, none of whom use the word "gumption," but without the support of an understanding family, great friends and helpful neighbors, well, there probably wouldn't be a race, would there? Many thanks to my wonderful wife Amy, my amazingly talented daughter Lauren, my mom Cindy and my in-laws Jerry and Alice, who have all been instrumental in putting me on the precipice of fulfilling my deranged dream. I hope every TD racer has a support crew as awesome as mine. Also, a special thanks to Yoda, the greatest philosopher of whatever century he lived in or still lives in, in wraith form. "Do, or do not do...there is no try." Totally.

Chasing Mary

Stephen Gleasner

I am still on the Divide. And I need to stop.

One month, I told my wife. But I left long before it started. Now it's done, and I am still not back.

On day 20 I cried so hard when "Treetop Flier" came on my Ipod that I had to pull over to the side of the trail. I thought my throat would close up and I would die out there between Platoro and Horca. Cried. A song about a drug-smuggling pilot. I felt like the smuggler, selfish, alone, gambling for the hollow buzz. Throwing dice on credit just to stay at the table.

But I have not had my run-in yet, my dairy dilemma in Horca, my confrontation with that little boy, in the store that shared its entryway with a church. Look left—pews, a pulpit, a wall-mounted Jesus. Right— a store, starkly lit, sparsely stocked.

He sat at the register, engrossed in the small world of his video game. My interruption drew him out, changed his focal length, made him squint fierce at me through his glasses. I reminded myself of what he saw—the crazy middle-aged man, helmet still on his head. The spandex fashion show. The mossy-toothed, sleep-deprived, last-place racer, amped-up and twitchy, looking for ice cream.

Ice cream. On a stick. For the call-in.

My vision— one foot kicked up against the wall and me with my one handed ice cream, on the payphone calling the race hotline to tell the world about my life since Del Norte. But the ice cream had melted, crawled halfway out of its half-assed chocolate sarcophagus before refreezing, leaving the stick buried in frozen goop.

Not a one-handed operation.

This would involve groveling, dog-licking the wrapper. Not part of my call-in vision. I stopped mid-dial. Stormed past Jesus. Presented the ice cream on the counter, a real piece of performance art.

"That ice cream is fine," he said after he inventoried the parts.

I flashed.

"Not fine. Melted. If you think that thing is fine, then you eat it.

My anger surprised me. It wasn't about the ice cream.

I left the church/store, felt better outside with room to breathe and sun on my face. Called-in to tell of the 14,000 feet of climbing since Del Norte yesterday afternoon. About my ice cream debacle. About the ladies at the Platoro store. They had a list of riders still on the trail. Everyone stops in Platoro if the store is open.

They were looking for Siren Mary. I was looking for her too.

I had seen Mary three times—the racer's meeting, the start, and for the beginning of the race, in the neutral zone where all the racers rode together for the first couple miles. Then Mary turned her head to the side, and blew first one nostril, then the other, violent, fast, done. It seemed as much a statement of purpose, a declaration of badassness, as it did a nose blowing. That one gesture told me that I didn't belong here. I thought about the six Q-tips in my pack, for after showers. About the baby wipes in my toilet kit. About the tube of Boudreaux's Butt Paste.

Then she stood up and rode away. I saw something blur by on her right calf. A tattoo.

She's twenty something, about 5'2", red hair, freckles surrounding her sun-faded tattoo. I have been tracking her since Banff, more than two thousand miles. She rides Kenda tires. Small Block Eights. I saw her last some twenty days ago.

Everyone stops in Platoro, to grab something to eat, so where was Mary?

Siren Mary.

Cordillera

She did Richmond Peak in the dark. That place slapped my soul in the day. I got lost post-holing in the snow up there, dragging my bike as I trudged. Mary did it in the dark. Bad-Bear country. Up high. In the snow. Where they bring the bears that can't behave in Yellowstone.

Mary. Damn it. Siren Mary and her small block eights. Tracks in mud, dried. Tracks in snow, vague. Mary and the lines she takes. The tracks back up the nose-blow— fast, efficient, hard-core.

I feel like a pervert tracking her. I have two kids and a wife at home. But I chase Mary. I cry most days at some point. But when I cry I am not sad. Stuff just washes over me, big waves of stuff, and tears break loose. I miss my wife and kids. I cry about this huge gift they have given me, "Go do this thing, and come back to us," my wife Illya said. Mostly the tears are forged in the crucible of gratitude, that my family understood my silly dream.

I am forty-six, on a bicycle, racing in the Tour Divide bike race, off-road, through the Rockies from Banff, Alberta to the Mexican border shack of Antelope Wells. I have been in last place for most of the month. Every time I pass someone and get out of last place that person curls up and dies.

Dave Nice, his fixed gear bike, his bloody sputum, his final call-in broken up with wheezing fits of coughing (his third race attempt).

Andy Buchanan crawled from a restaurant white-faced— coughing so hard he thought he would die. Crawled out (his second attempt).

The first Kevin just went home. Something about a job interview. And up in front, they take buses home. Hitch rides.

The other Kevin, The Kevinator spooled it up good. Exploded roadside with a frozen Achilles. Could not ride or walk. Hit the 911 button on his transponder (his third race attempt).

First place, Ruben, blew up sky-high in Colorado. His knee and ankle swelled up huge, no longer able to bend. Bus-ride.

But I am here. I ride every day, passing the ghosts of dropped racers. Chasing Siren Mary. My wife knows. She tells me where Mary is when my cell works.

"You almost caught her last night," she said. "But Mary kept riding".

I cry every time on the phone. She can't hear it, the fist in my throat. No sound comes from me. I shouldn't be here. I should be in Maine cutting the grass, painting the house.

Before I left I made lawn arrangements with Dave across the street.

"I will cut it like it was my own," he said.

Dave's lawn mower broke so he let our lawn go hayfield just like his.

I ride into the open, into this bigness, where guys shoot rifles with beer can diameter scopes from truck hoods at small animals invisible in the distance. In this open sage country failure hits hard, clings like burdocks to a wool sweater. Thunderheads move like killer jellyfish. They stack and go dark and flat on the bottom. Hen's bottoms. Nesting feathers of electrical destruction. They move this way and that. Capricious. I pedal faster. 12, 13, 14 miles per hour, reaching deep for the extra speed to keep safe from lightning. Show God some effort, maybe He will spare me.

And then the news—that butcher up the street is cutting my grass, his riding mower, his camouflaged hat, his coffee stained mustache, no upper lip visible. He cuts our grass while his oiled wife tans out by their clothesline, reading romances and getting pissed at him and the din of his tractor in my yard.

And I ride all day, every day. Banff is three thousand miles from Maine. Every day I ride farther from home—heading to that Mexican border shack. Antelope Wells.

I have crossed over the Continental Divide too many times. I am just along for the ride now, broken and crying at the mountains standing in the quiet of evening, the colors draped on the snow covered peaks. It seems like too much beauty for just one person.

Opulence.

I cry that I still ride. I cry for the people I met at the start, had breakfast with, who have dropped from the route. Shattered Divide dreams.

I am out past the breakers. Just like I always joked about, but now it's real. Grappling- hook-on-my-soul-real. Now I am in the deep water where only the big waves break, out past the lineup. Alone.

I still have a family— at least I think I do. Maybe I have been on this trail forever.

Dinner in El Rito, just before Abiquiu, in an alley next to Martins, the grocery/auto parts/hardware place. One part of the burrito is frozen. Crystalline. The other part blistered the roof of my mouth. Microwave perfection.

Cordillera

Anything wrong with the mouth is serious. Have to eat. Lots everyday. The burrito burn will go well with the sores on my lips. Taking a large bite of anything means breaking open the sores again.

A kid on a dirt bike goes by. He should have shifted already but runs it up, as he blasts downtown El Rito. A blue cloud follows, small at the pipe, and then relaxing, an oily sigh, growing, reclining like a genie out of its bottle.

A woman in a sagging car with mismatched wheels, lurches to a slanted halt next to the payphone, leaving the rear of the car in the road. The car bobs to a stop. Dead shocks. Her hysterical Spanish, crying, shrieking into the black receiver when the dirt bike kid smokes by, the rich blue plume adding another layer of smoke.

Dinner in the alley.

The blister inflates, a large peaceful bubble on the roof of my mouth.

She was here. Mary. The clerk told me she bought a burrito. Hour ago.

In the alley I chew and worry about the blister. The grass is tall in clumps with sand and broken glass between. Mary, an hour ahead. The smell of the blue smoke, pungent. I taste oil with the doming blister.

I call home. Try to stay objective. Location. What I am eating. Don't tell them how much I miss them. Keep the hatches closed, so my damaged emotional submarine doesn't fill with water and sink to the bottom.

The sun is getting low, a warm evening glow. The air is comfortable.

The dead town is alive with motorized little kid and the woman, her forehead against the black and chrome of the phone, and her Spanish lilt running high and fast, summoning some ancient spirit.

"What's that sound," asks my wife.

"El Rito. It sounds like that here."

And the cell drops. Great Divide reception.

And I call back. Battery low. Always low now. Never more than a bar or two of power. The solar charger can't keep up.

My wife can see my location on the computer in our bedroom in Maine.

I call back. The kid on the bike takes the Spanish lady to a new level. The 2-cycle echos off the old brick and dusty glass of the crumbling town. Now she is shrieking and crying into the receiver and its chrome tether. I have no tether. I am solar, unplugged, barely connected.

"Clark has something to tell you...."

I have not spoken to him for weeks. His eight-year-old voice is higher than I remember.

"Guess what dad?"

And the connection breaks.

I stuff the whole frozen section of the burrito in, hear the crunch of crystals, and feel them press on the blister, a tight inverted dome.

The blue smoke goes by. The Spanish lady screams at the sky, her head back, arms to the clouds. Gravity pulls at her parts under her t-shirt. Broken glass at the base of the buildings on both sides of my dining alley, punctuation for drinks finished. Nowhere to sit, bars low on the phone. I tongue at the tight pillow of fluid on the roof of my mouth, covered with the chalk of frozen burrito. I call back.

Illya answers.

"Put Clark on."

"Guess what dad?"

My cell drops again.

The lady sobs quietly, leaning against the building. The motorcycle kid has disappeared, but I still taste the smoke, the blue still hangs in neat layers.

I lean my bike. Put my stiff leg over. Look at the map. I have doubts about it.

Again.

I ask someone outside the store. Show them the map. Wrinkled brows. Then they always want to hold the map, unfold it, been this way since day one, this battle with the map, the locals having never heard of that road...behind that outhouse, that turns to a goat trail.

"Where do you wanna go?" they ask.

"Let me see that map of yours. I lived here all my life. Never heard of that road....."

I leave the noise, and blue smoke plume that now hangs in silent stratified layers. The phone lady sobs, lets the receiver dangle from its cord. I ride into the open, alone into the high desert, so I can cry by myself. Cry for the mesas, the evening light on them. Cry for my wife and the growing grass. Cry for the Jesus still crucified back there in Horca, with his florescent view of my friend playing his video games, sneering like a hyena at the clientele and their ruined ice cream treats. To weep for that woman, her car, her shattered life, the dangling receiver, and the voice on the other end.

At least this mesa light show is paved. I smell the spice of dry desert death, a rawhide cow, dry and hollow, still in the posture of its last moment. Now a shelter to mice.

Abiquiu.

Every wagon wheel leaned up against every shack catches my eye.

I look for Mary and her big wheels. A dark wet spot on side of the road from Mary, peeing out here in the wide open, with the mesas looking on. She must be close.

The sun lowers. The vulnerable time of day. Beautiful. I have no destination other than to ride on into this cartoon desert scene. See if I can catch Mary.

"Mary doesn't want you to catch her," said a woman a day ago at a camp in the Cruces Basin, "She said to give you lots of beer. She was just here. Rode off into the night after we fed her dinner." I ate the ribs and corn they offered, drank one beer, made camp for the night next to them.

I have a family. I should be back in Maine, cutting the grass. Painting the house. Illya loves our house. Our family. We have two cats and 10 laying hens. Talk of a puppy soon. We have a play set in the backyard. Illya's gardens keep track of time with colors. My cluttered studio, a space I know well enough to walk in darkness to the light switch on the far wall. Clark and Meg. The names of their stuffed animals. Clark and his night terrors. Meg and her music box dance. Her messy art table. The miles of cutting she has done with her scissors.

I might have made all this up, this elaborate back-story for this broken rider, something to fill this emptiness of always moving, always wind in my ears. I might have made up this race, this orange satellite transponder, more fiction to back up this nomadic life. I am pretty sure this all started in Banff a couple weeks ago, but it's getting harder to convince myself that it isn't just some sort of made-up survival mechanism.

Then, up ahead, in the dry expanse, I see something, a bike coming onto the road, those meager packs, it is a Divide machine.

Siren Mary.

So many weeks ago she rode away, so many stories from people, about Mary, and now this is Mary, sores around her mouth, just like mine. I have her Croc lashed to the top of my pack. I found it roadside this morning. Remembered it from Banff at the start, strapped to the top of her pack. She laughs. A sore-cracking laugh.

"I threw the other one out in Vallecitos," she says snapping a picture of her missing blue sandal lashed to the top of my stuff.

I brought it as a peace offering, to soften the blow of catching her. Roadside with one foot down, words fly. Plans.

She tells me of Abiquiu. The store closes in a half hour. She has a room for the night, a hacienda. The restaurant is good. Pasta. We will hit the trail early. I like the plan, but, roadside, it feels abrupt.

I want a bed, I want to stomp my clothes clean as I shower. I want safety, sleep. I don't know Mary. I'm not sure I know myself anymore. Maybe the hotel is not a good idea.

Siren Mary. Copyright Stephen Gleasner.

Cordillera

I have a plane to catch out of El Paso, and I am running behind schedule, but if I can finish with Mary her crew can take my bike, ship it home for me, and I can get a ride from Antelope Wells to El Paso. Time is critical. I need this to make my flight. If I finish by myself I will not make my flight. If I ride by myself I will need to bail out in Silver City. Just another Divide DNF. Silver City is only 125 miles short of finishing.

I go with Mary to the store. I pretend that I know what I want, but I watch Mary. Her junk food choices are better than mine. I quietly put things back replace them with her better ideas. In the checkout she eyes my food on the grocery belt, identical to hers, says nothing.

Back at the hotel, I call home. The western sun is down now. Clark is on Maine time, asleep for hours.

"What did he want to tell me, the important thing?"

"He lost his front tooth."

Silence.

The fist in my throat tightens. The blood rushes to my face.

"Can you hear me?"

"I can't talk, gotta go." I hang up.

"News from home?" Mary asks.

I start to tell Mary of Clark's tooth and the phone, but I have to stop.

She fills my silence, "You want coffee in the morning?"

I stomp my clothes clean in the shower. Incredible dirt leaves an alluvial fan of grit in the tub.

I use my last Q-tip.

Sleep sits heavy like a lead X-ray vest. More a constriction of all senses than sleep. That Divide disappearing act that happens every night.

Sleep. A deep darkness that suffocates dreams and makes you wonder about the void and where the dreams went. Maybe they went to some poolside Florida timeshare. But the Divide doesn't leave anything extra for the dreams to feed on. Dream chemo.

An alarm goes off in the middle of the night. I start rolling my bag on the floor. Gathering my stuff hanging from every hook, rod, and light fixture, drying. The room is filled with our damp clothes that get compressed into packs.

Mary makes coffee. The aroma fills the small room, the reassuring sound of the coffee maker's final sputter.

Coffee ready. It seems out of place with this nomadic life. As we pack the bikes outside, clips and zippers shatter the dark desert stillness.

The air is cold. I feel strong. She matches my pace.

I see the tattoo on her calf in the town's last streetlight. In the dark, climbing out of town, I ask what it is.

She's quiet for a moment.

"It was a mistake. I made a trade."

I don't want to know about the trade.

Our headlights tangle as we climb the dirt road out of town.

Her voice comes from beside me in the dark.

"It's a fairy."

Crossing The Divide

Glenn Stalgren

By day seven of the 2009 Tour Divide bike race, I was ready to give up. I'd been sleeping only five, fitful hours a night. A kink in my neck kept me from turning my head to the left, and a pain shot to my fingertips whenever I tried. My diet had become that of an eighth-grader. It was all crackers and candy, and my GI tract betrayed the strain. I no longer had bowel movements, only intermittent spasms. My head was foggy, and my grip on reality was weakening. I wanted to stop. But the race continued, and so did I.

At this point, I should confess that my wretched state and the Tour Divide were all but unrelated; I wasn't actually racing a mountain bike along the Continental Divide. Rather, my suffering sprang from my sick infant son, his discomfort and, more to the point, his willingness to share it with his mother and me. During the 2009 Tour Divide, my son simultaneously endured *another* ear infection, the eruption of molar teeth and a spectacular diarrheal infection. This trifecta of *ears, tears, and smears* kept him from going to the babysitter… so it was Daddy day care for the shrieking, teeth gnashing, sewer mutant. Lucky me.

Although I accomplished very little that second week in June that didn't involve bleeding gums or diarrhea, I occasionally found time to visit the Tour Divide website. A friend was in the race and his suffering was a temporary shelter from my offspring's snot storm. *Misery loves company*, they say, and I found my companions on the Tour Divide's Leaderboard. Every morning I looked forward to reading about the Divide Racers who, I loved to assume, were even more miserable than me.

What will it be today? I often asked while firing up the Tour Divide homepage and drumming my fingers together. I was frankly giddy at the prospect of finding comfort in the challenges of Divide Racing: hand-to-hand grizzly combat, gouty testicular swelling and tales of racers hungry enough to eat scavenged deer droppings. On top of my wish list was a *Racer Update* consisting of only four words: "The horror! The *horror!*" Oh, I wished for that.

It was shallow and selfish. It was infant induced *schadenfrued*, plain and simple. I felt better because somewhere out there Divide Racers were feeling worse.

Kurt Refsnider suffers on The Divide in 2009. Copyright Eddie Clark

But it didn't last, by the second week of the race, my son began to improve… his otic inflammation retreated, his molars ended their assault, and torpedoes appeared in his pants again. We resumed playing together at the beach, laughing and pushing his toy trucks around. As my son improved, I began to heal as well.

My interest in the race changed too. It happened sometime during that second week, when I was hunched over my laptop eagerly expecting a daily dose of Divide Racing gloom. Like the Grinch of Whoville expecting misery but instead finding joy, I was startled to read of sublime delight on The Divide. *What is this?* Despite the bleeding, the aching muscles and the weighty sense of an eternal challenge, racers seemed to be enjoying themselves. It was an epiphany; rather than searching for misery, I scanned the reports for joy and redemption on The Divide. I lived vicariously through strangers and rooted for racers that I'd never heard of *–go Jill, faster Matthew, spin it to win it Deanna you crazy hipster!*

There was constant movement on the Leaderboard as racers dropped out or fell back. I felt helpless whenever someone scratched; I wanted to comfort them, to send a sympathy card and give the smelly, unwashed hero a quick thumbs up from safely across the room. For a few days in late June it appeared that illness, injury, and flooding would wipe out the entire field but through it all joyful updates continued to flow over the Internet. Some riders coalesced into informal pelotons while others pushed on as lone wolves in spandex. All had the pretense of a comfortable life scrubbed away and, in the process, found some kernel of redemption on The Divide. Watching their transformation was rejuvenating.

All the drama on The Divide made me wonder: "Who came up with such a brilliant recipe for suffering and misery?" The challenges along a Divide Race are legendary: 2745+ miles of mucky, unimproved roads, over 200,000 vertical feet of elevation gain, route navigation, all of it without any assistance. I imagined the possibilities: was it an austere sect of self-flagellating monks who discovered the route. Was it a Roman sadist or the Prince of Darkness himself?

Of course, John Stamstad was the first to race the Great Divide Mountain Bike Route; throwing down a super human time of just over eighteen days. Then came Mike Curiak and the Great Divide Race, followed by the Tour Divide itself. But who rode the route first? Who had the guts and creativity to bike the spine of our country before anyone else, before the GDMBR and before even the first Divide Race?

Buried in the Internet is the answer: Mike and Dan Moe. The brothers from Laramie, Wyoming rode their bicycles along the Continental Divide in 1984. As far as history can tell, they were the first to complete the entire route by bike. The Moes were exceptional adventurers; creative, strong and humble. The Moes rode The Divide in reverse (as it would be described today) from Mexico to Canada, unsupported, with only a compass and hundred year old maps to guide them. They were often forced to take a bearing and backtrack; it was the kind of intensive, methodical route finding that would make a modern Divide Racer go bananas.

During their ride, Mike Moe observed that, "We sometimes find ourselves facing a stretch of country without any type of trail or road." Rather than lament these difficulties, the Moes chalked them up as "the charm of The Divide." Rumor has it that their feat, published in a now defunct bicycling magazine, inspired Michael McCoy to spend years mapping what would become the Great Divide Mountain Bike Route, Divide Racing's official course. Racers and fans alike owe a great deal to the Moe brothers.

Much has changed since the Moe's bushwhacking tour. Today racers follow at least a hint of a trail over the entire course and race for speed on machines that the Moes would scarcely recognize. Perhaps, as a penalty for these luxuries, an additional 250 Canadian miles have been added to create the Great Divide Mountain Bike Route as it is today; apparently one nation isn't challenge enough to truly test a Divide Racer's mettle. Divide Racers also compete in categories that would confound the Moe brothers who toured on basic steel bikes. There's a *Single Speed* category. I suppose this is for those who feel that a derailleur confers an unfair advantage. There's also a *Fixie* category. I guess some racers think that even going downhill should be grueling. *Why stop there?* How about a *Flat-Tire* category, to exorcise the demons of inflated inner tubes? And the June start time seems like cheating too, doesn't it? Why not have the race begin with the first major snowstorm of the winter. Or possibly, a strictly-enforced no-eating-or-drinking rule along the route? But that's the old me, the bitter me talking.

I continued following the 2009 racers as they trickled across the finish line at Antelope Wells, New Mexico. While some vowed never to race again, others promised to return another year. Three weeks prior, in the depths of the misery I shared with my son, I couldn't have fathomed that desire. But today it seems reasonable. I even catch myself envying the racers, the same poor souls I had nothing but pity for in early June. *Maybe I could enter the race next year*, I wonder sometimes, *with my son in a bike seat!* That could be a new category! Hey Matthew Lee, what do you think?

When I mention it to my wife, she answers with silence and takes our son out of the room.

My racer friend reached the finish in twenty one days, but I continued to follow the race until the last racer reached Antelope Wells nearly 32 days after the start. I've never met Michael Komp, but I was rooting for him until the last second. What a race!

Mike and Dan Moe met their tragic end a million miles from the Great Divide in the Arctic Ocean. They never saw their original ride along The Divide grow into the world's toughest bike race. Sometimes I wonder what they would think about modern Divide Racing. Would they enter the Tour Divide? Would they scoff at the relative ease of the modern race; with its detailed maps and satellite tracking?

The Moe brothers took over two months to complete the US section of The Divide, the winner of this year's Tour Divide finished that portion in less than 17 days. I have a feeling that the Moes would at least be saddened by the unrelenting focus on speed. Surely Mike and Dan would feel a sense of loss, of melancholy, over the changes on The Divide itself. The Divide is no longer the wild and remote place it once was. But the Moes were pioneers; they did things the hard way so that others could stand on their shoulders. That's the way of The Great Divide, it always has been. I think that Mike and Dan would understand.

The End

Mark Jenkins

Editor's Note: Like Divide Racers dashing through small towns at night, Mike and Dan Moe have appeared in the Cordillera without warning or context. The Moe brothers were possibly the first to ride the entire Continental Divide. They did it in 1984, on rudimentary machines when The Divide was much wilder. In this final Cordillera piece Mark Jenkins, a writer for National Geographic, touches on the life and death of the brothers who inspired the Great Divide Mountain Bike Route. This piece was published in Mark's book A Man's Life, Dispatches from Dangerous Places.

The water is so cold that icebergs are floating in the middle. It's June in Wyoming, at 11,000 feet, and Lookout Lake is only half melted out. The snow is still five feet deep along the shore, and chunks have calved into the water.

Mike Moe and I have hiked in to climb the Diamond, a 600-foot quartzite face in the Medicine Bow Mountains. People rarely climb here—it's too high, too harsh, too dangerous. There are often snow squalls, rockfall, route-finding debacles. Mike and I have been climbing the Diamond for 20 years; it's where we train for epics. This summer we're going on separate expeditions to Canada: Mike to attempt a ski traverse of Baffin Island; me to try a new route on Mount Waddington. This is our last chance to climb together.

Cordillera

Scrambling through the jagged terrain down to Lookout Lake, I feel nimble and at ease. We've done this so many times before, it's as though I'm sliding back through time.

At the water's edge, Mike leaps out onto a flat rock and begins to strip. He stuffs his socks into his boots, wraps his shirt in his trousers, and plugs it all inside his backpack. Then he stands there naked, stroking his short red beard, contemplating the still, black water.

The surface of the lake is a mirror, perfectly reflecting Medicine Bow Peak and its series of stone faces. Here, at the bottom of the mountain, we are still in night's shadow, but dawn is beginning to gild the summit. Long, pink clouds, like giant rainbow trout, suddenly appear in the water. Except the trout are swimming upside down above a mountain that is pointing inward instead of upward. It is a surreal reflection—as if we're looking at the other side of life.

"Last one to the other side . . ." Mike says, and dives into the lake.

At that moment, a scene from another time fills my mind.

Diving in from the vine bridge, Mike was immediately swept out of sight. The huge brown river just took him. It had been pouring buckets in Guinea for months and the Niger was swollen fat as a snake that's swallowed a goat, and we couldn't tell how many trees had been pulled into the water that might trap us in our kayaks, so Mike said he'd swim the river to find out. Use his body as a proxy for us and our boats. "It's the only way to test it," he'd insisted. It was the fall of 1991 and his wife was pregnant and my wife was pregnant and we were in Africa hoping to pull off one last big expedition before life changed for good.

He's done this before, but it still stuns me. The water is so cold it would instantly paralyze anyone but Mike. Will alone keeps him warm.

I grab his pack and begin hopping boulder to boulder through the snowfield. This is our ritual. I'll hike around the lake, he'll swim across it. We'll meet on the far side, just north of the Diamond.

It's getting light now and the air is a cool violet. I can see Mike chopping through icy water, his feet fluttering. Unlike me, he is utterly unafraid of water. It is his natural element. In high school he was a state-champion swimmer.

I meet him on the far shore. When he comes out of the water, he's so frozen his skin is a waxy, translucent blue and his movements jerky. His jaw is clenched and he can't speak, but he's grinning. He fumbles putting his clothes back on; I have to tie his boot laces for him because his fingers are wooden. Heaving on our packs, we continue up through the talus, across a hard tongue of snow.

Mike is a wit, peculiarly quick-minded. He has an ever-changing repertoire of voices, a dozen nicknames for me. We rarely get the chance to go into the mountains together anymore, so when we do, we gleefully revert to our younger, bolder selves.

At the base of the Diamond, Mike stacks the rope and, finally able to talk, says, "Suppose you think you're leading."

We both want to lead—it has been this way since the beginning—but, eager beaver that I am, I already have my rock shoes on. I point to them.

"I see, Rhubarb the Black's got 'iz scuppers on already," says Mike in his pirate's brogue. "Then the sharp end be yours."

Mike and I gravitated to each other as teenagers. We both lived on the edge of Laramie, the boundless prairie our backyard. We were predetermined to be wild and became perfectly matched partners in misadventure: Mike and Mark. Climbing came naturally to us, and we scaled everything in sight. University buildings, boulders, smokestacks, mountain walls—our adolescent enthusiasm and daring far exceeding our ability. Soon enough even wide-open Wyoming started feeling small. We lied about our ages, got jobs on the railroad, lived in a tent behind the Virginian Hotel in Medicine Bow, banked the cash, then left high school to spend half a year hitchhiking through Europe, Africa, and Russia, climbing and chasing girls. We got arrested in Tunisia, Luxembourg, and Leningrad. We got robbed. We slept in the dirt.

Through college at the University of Wyoming, Mike and I double-dated, debated Nietzsche, and stood back to back defending atheism, dismembering our Christian attackers with rapier tongues. We ice climbed and skied the backcountry and went on expeditions. Close calls were commonplace, and we thought nothing of them. We pushed each other but willingly stood in for the other whenever one of us was weak or scared or lost. We were outdoor brothers-in-arms. We would die for each other without flinching—and almost did a dozen times.

"You're on," Mike announces, and I start up a dihedral between the wall and a delicate pillar. The pillar—ten feet wide, ten feet thick, and 200 feet tall—leans precariously against the Diamond. We have used this route to gain the upper face multiple times, but it always feels dicey. We console ourselves with the fact that the pillar has stood here for thousands of years.

Today the crack is running with water and dangerously slippery. Halfway up I mention this fact.

"Is that whining I hear?" cries Mike in his Monty Python voice. "Courtesy slack coming your way."

We were 16 and just learning how to climb and we made a pact that whining was prohibited. No matter how freaked you were, you had to keep your mouth shut. To enforce this rule Mike came up with a penalty called "courtesy slack": The belayer fed out extra rope—so you'd take a longer fall—whenever even a whimper was heard. Over the years, this bred a black, Brit-like humor in Mike. The more desperate the situation, the more he made fun of it: "It's absolutely grand—no handholds whatsoever" or "If the ice were only a wee bit thinner and more rotten I could actually enjoy myself." We were ripe with hubris. As far as we could tell we were indestructible.

At the top of the pillar I move onto the wall, set up a belay, and Mike begins climbing. I notice that he moves more slowly than he used to, but then he doesn't climb so much anymore. He has other passions now.

After college, we both did big expeditions—I went to Shishapangma and Everest; Mike walked the Continental Divide with his younger brother, Dan, then two years later mountain-biked it—but our priorities were diverging. The year I went to Everest, 1986, Mike took an internship in Washington, D.C., working for the hunger-relief organization Bread for the World. In 1987, we both went to Africa. With my girlfriend, Sue Ibarra, I climbed Mount Kilimanjaro and Mount Kenya and traveled far and wide writing adventure stories. Mike went to Swaziland to work for CARE, teaching poor Swazis how to get small-business loans. He helped start a daycare center. His girlfriend, Diana Kocornik, was teaching in Swaziland for the Mennonite Central Committee. Mike started going to church.

We all moved back to Wyoming in 1990, bought houses, and started families. When I got married, Mike was my best man. At his wedding, I was a groomsman—his brother, Dan, was his best man. My daughter Addi and his son Justin were both born in January 1992; my daughter Teal and his twins, Carlie and Kevin, were born one month apart two years later. I kept writing stories; Mike took a job as the director of Wyoming Parent, a nonprofit family-advocate organization.

Halfway up the leaning pillar, he yells, "Wish it were wetter in here!"

Mike pulls himself up onto the top of the pillar and steps over to the belay.

"Mike, what if the pillar suddenly collapsed?" I ask.

"Won't," he says. "It's been here forever."

"But what if it did?"

"Buck, you'd catch me."

Mike is the most optimistic person I know. He is sanguine, imperturbable.

"What if you lost your ice ax?" Mike asked one day in 1979. "Could you still climb the couloir?" We were training for McKinley by climbing the snowy chutes on either side of the Diamond. So we tried it without our axes, scraping little holds in the snow with our woolen mittens. What if you lost your ice ax and crampons? I asked.

Could you still get up the couloir? We kicked tiny steps with our heavy leather boots and gouged mitten holes and climbed it. But what if you were descending? We practiced glissading with nothing to stop the death slide but a sharp rock in our hands.

Thus began our private game of what-if. What-if was meant to make us more resourceful, more capable of surviving desperate situations. And it did—for a time.

We swap leads and Mike moves out onto a sheet of gray rock split by a pencil-thin crack.

"But, Mike, what if I couldn't and you were killed? Was it worth it?" I'm baiting him and he knows it.

"Yup. Right up until the moment I die . . . then it's completely not worth it."

"That's not an answer and you know it."

The crack has closed off and Mike is holding on by his fingertips. He uses this predicament not to respond.

Our game of what-if was good fun for more than a decade, but it changed after we had kids. Before, we always assumed we'd come home. That was the principle of what-if. What if this or that happened—how would you get yourself out of the fix? But after kids, we both began to wonder what if . . . we didn't? What if we were killed? By a grizzly, by a river, by a collapsing pillar of stone. It's a natural thing to ask once you start thinking about someone besides yourself. We may be leaving on expeditions to Canada soon, but we are dads now, not Huck and Tom. Justin and Addi are three years old; Teal and Carlie and Kevin will turn one this summer. Our game of what-if has evolved into the fundamental conundrum of our lives: Is it morally possible to be a serious adventurer and a father?

For my part, I hide behind the hackneyed and sophistic excuse that it's who I am. That if I were to quit adventuring, I wouldn't be Mark Jenkins—which I know is bullcrap. People change all the time and don't lose their identity. They often become someone better. I just don't have the willpower.

Mike does. He's been trying to reform himself for years. He's weaning himself off adventure like a heavy drinker weans himself off Scotch. Slowly, with frequent relapses. He has promised Diana—and himself—he will do only one big trip every two years, but I sense this expedition to Baffin will be his last. Inside, I know Mike believes serious adventure, expeditioning, is incompatible with being a father—you are imperiling not simply your own life but the lives of your children, which is immoral. So he will have to give it up.

To calm his existential qualms, Mike has taken to putting more and more effort into planning the logistics of an expedition. This upcoming trip to Canada is a case in point. He's spent weeks testing gear, studying maps, developing contingencies. He told me he thinks he can bring the risk down to something acceptable. I told him he's in denial. Risk is integral to adventure. A freak accident, an unanticipatable rockslide, an avalanche. No risk, no adventure. He knows this, but he's torn between being the man he is and the man he believes he should be.

I feel a tug on the rope and look up. Mike is far above his last piece of protection, and the crack has vanished. There are no handholds and nothing to stand on. Most climbers would back down.

"Watch me!" Mike yells, and dives for a thin ledge.

A letter arrived for me from Swaziland. It was 1989 and I was in Novosibirsk, crossing Siberia by bicycle. Mike wrote, "Dear Dostoyevsky the Big Legs—expect you have saddle sores the size of rubles and lungs like a hippo but the KGB has no doubt caught you by now so I'll soon be mounting a daring rescue . . ." He went on for several paragraphs in his clumsy handwriting and terrible spelling, and between the lines I knew he was worried about me and that he was really saying he would do anything for me, march to the ends of the earth if I needed him. I missed him so much I reread the letter over and over, asking myself why I never told him how much he meant to me, why I never just told him I loved him.

Mike barely catches the lip of rock.

He belays me up and I lead the final pitch. We're 800 feet above Lookout Lake, but the climbing is relaxing and fun. Mike got the sketchy pitch, the bastard. I realize now that that's why he didn't argue for the first lead.

I reach the summit, lean against a warm slab of rock, bring Mike up, and we sit there side by side, staring out across Wyoming.

"Mike, remember Lhasa?"

He grins, but I can tell it's really a grimace.

We went to Tibet in 1993 to climb an unknown peak, and after two days in Lhasa Mike got pulmonary edema, just like he did when we were on McKinley, except there was no way to go down and his lungs filled up with fluid, and we went to the hospital, but they could only give him a Chinese army balloon of oxygen that he sucked on while we waited for the plane. His lungs were gurgling so badly he couldn't lie down, so he had to sit up all night, but even then he was still drowning from the inside. His face was bloated and gray, and if the plane didn't come in the morning he would die, but he was the funniest he'd ever been. He kept making me laugh, and I was so scared I was sick to my stomach, and when I heard the sound of the plane I began to weep.

Atop the Diamond, feet dangling in space, we are on the roof of our world. We eat the lunches our wives have packed for us and silently observe the landscape that made us: snow and ice and rock and sky. We sit there together for a long time, feeling as close as we ever have.

After a while we coil the rope and pack up the gear and begin discussing our upcoming expeditions. I'm going to Waddington with my friend John Harlin. It took a lot of persuading. His father died climbing the Eiger, and John has spent much of his adult life struggling with what that means. In his early twenties, John had a partner who died while they were descending from British Columbia's Mount Robson. After that, he promised his wife, Adele, and his mother that he would give up alpinism. Going to Waddington with me means he's breaking his promise.

Mike will attempt to ski across the Barnes Ice Cap on Baffin Island with his brother, Dan, and two other good friends of ours, Brad Humphrey and Sharon Kava. I have tried to convince Sharon not to go—I worry that she doesn't have the experience for an Arctic trip—but Mike's enthusiasm is magnetic. It is something we disagree on. Mike believes that self-confidence and sangfroid—both of which he has an abundance of—are more valuable than technical ability. I don't.

I ask him what he fears most.

Mike Moe. Copyright Mark Jenkins.

"Same as ever, bro."

Years ago, Mike confided that his deepest fear was that something would happen to his brother Dan while they were on a trip together. Dan, quiet and happy, the kid who fainted during sex-ed films in junior high, a man who has never said a bad word about anyone, has always looked up to Mike. Mike is the natural-born leader, Dan the disciple.

"I couldn't bear it," Mike whispers.

To descend, we walk along the edge of the Diamond, passing right by where the plaque will be, but of course it's not there yet.

We mounted the plaque in the summer of 1996. Tim Banks and Keith Spenser and I—Mike's closest friends—climbed the Diamond at midnight in honor of Mike's motto, "Any real adventure begins and ends in the dark." I led and Keith carried the engraved metal plaque, heavy as a headstone, in his pack, while Tim hiked around the back side to the summit. Halfway up, at about 3 A.M., Keith and I were shocked by little orange explosions all around us. Keith thought someone was using a night scope to shoot at us and this seemed insane but the cracking was everywhere and then we smelled it and realized they were firecrackers. Tim was throwing bottle rockets down at us, hooting with laughter. We finished bolting the plaque to the summit block right as the sun came up.

On the hike down from the Diamond, Mike is talking about changing the world, as usual. He's been reading the research. Most kids with problems come from single-parent families. As director of Wyoming Parent, he plans to change this. He's got some ideas, but he needs state funding. He knows he can get it. He believes in legislation. He believes in laws that encourage citizens and companies to act in the best interest of the community. He believes in the basic goodness of people.

I'm listening, but I don't have Mike's faith. I used to, but I've spent too much time in screwed-up countries. I've spent too much time in places where evil things happen purely because of evil people.

In 1998 I awoke in a black, hot, locked room in northern Burma and realized I'd been dreaming about Mike every night for weeks. I desperately needed his companionship and judgment because things were getting perilous and if he'd been with me we would have balanced each other and I wouldn't have gone off the rails, or better yet I wouldn't have even come to Burma.

We've dropped down the back of the Diamond and swung around to Lake Marie and we're sloshing back through the snow to the car.

"What do you say we take Justin and Addi up here this winter?" Mike says. "Build a snow cave, teach them how to wipe with snow, howl with the wind."

I tell Mike I'm in, of course.

It was late August of 1995 and Diana and the kids were over at our house for a backyard barbecue and we were all eagerly speculating about when Mike and Dan and Sharon and Brad would be home because it would be anytime now. Later that evening Diana called and her voice was so strange I didn't recognize it. She asked us to come over to her house, and when I walked in the door Perry and Greta, Mike and Dan's parents, were sitting stone still on the couch, and I knew immediately and my legs failed me and I dropped to my knees.

The telephone rang. It was the Royal Canadian Mounted Police out of Clyde River, Northwest Territories. Diana asked me to speak to them. I couldn't speak, so I just listened.

The team had successfully crossed Baffin Island, the expedition was over, and they were on their way home. They were coming back across Baffin Bay in a small aluminum motorboat with an Inuit guide named Jushua. They saw a pod of bowhead whales among the icebergs, and then the whales disappeared beneath the black water. Then one breached right under their boat and flipped it over. They were two miles from shore and couldn't right the craft because of the plywood steering shed. Jushua was wearing a marine survival suit, but the team had only life jackets.

On the way home from the Diamond, Mike drives. I shove in an old cassette tape I find on the passenger seat. Turns out to be Abbey Road. We know every song by heart. "Come Together," "Here Comes the Sun," "Golden Slumbers," "The End." We sing along like we have on so many road trips. I take bass and Mike sings tenor, slipping into falsetto just to make me laugh. We think we sound terrific. We sing at the top of our lungs. "And in the end, the love you take is equal to the love you make."

Jushua was found alive, washed ashore after 18 hours in the sea. He said they held hands across the hull of the boat for as long as they could, but the water was so cold. Mike was encouraging them all and cracking jokes and reassuring them that the mighty Mounties would be sending out a search flight any minute and to just hold on, just hold on. After a while Mike was the only one who could still talk.

First Sharon slipped away, face down in the water, then Brad. Dan and Mike held on to each other, hands clasped over the hull, for six hours. Then Dan began to slip away and Mike tried to grab him, tried to hold on to his brother, but he couldn't. Mike clung to the upturned boat for two more hours, talking to himself, going mad, before floating away into the Arctic. He was 37.

When the tape ends Mike and I stop singing and are quiet for a spell. Just driving across the high plains, antelope in the distance, wind combing the tall brown grass.

It was October that same year and snowing and we were below the Diamond and I was trembling holding Justin's tiny hand as he threw the ashes. Perry would never accept the death of his sons and died of heartbreak three years later. I'd see Greta alone in the park and we'd just hold hands and cry.

Cordillera

Years later, none of us were the same or ever could be, and the shock and despair now blessedly came only in the middle of the night. And on one of those nights in the dead of winter the giant pillar leaning against the Diamond collapsed and shattered into a thousand pieces, but the plaque we'd mounted on the summit in memory of Mike and Dan and Brad and Sharon is still there.

Eleven years after they froze to death in the Arctic Ocean, I called Diana to tell her I was writing this story. She said Justin and Carlie and Kevin would have been such different people, and we both broke down on the phone.

Then she said: "But, Mark, there are so many ways to lose your life besides dying."

As we glide into Laramie we're talking about our kids. Mike and I have big plans. As soon as they're a little older we'll take them climbing at Devils Tower, like we did together when we were young. We'll take them cross-country skiing in Yellowstone so they can sit in the hot pools like we did. We'll teach them to climb Fear and Loathing, a face route that is all about balance, about deftly moving on invisible edges, never thinking about falling, and believing with all your heart that you can stand on air.

About the Authors

Jon Billman writes for such magazines as Outside and Mountain Bike. He lives with his family in False Creek, Oklahoma.

Eric Bruntjen is the Editor of the Cordillera. He lives in central Washington with his wife Melanee, son Win and daughter Ona.

Cadet Bryant is a team rider and ultra-distance runner for Ellsworth Handcrafted Bicycles. He resides in West Texas with his dog of eleven years, a Queensland Blue Heeler named Molly, who is his best friend and dedicated running partner. He has taught English within the Texas public school system for seven years (and has coached girl's athletics) at the junior high and high school levels. Currently, Cadet is taking a break from the bike and pursuing his first love that developed during childhood— running. He has placed well in numerous fifty-mile trail runs across the country, even shutting out horses in Prescott, Arizona's, infamous "Man against Horse" race. He will compete in his second one-hundred mile run in Philadelphia during the spring of 2010 and plans to ferociously pursue a top overall placing in the 2010 Montrail Ultra Cup.

Diana C. Gleasner is a travel writer living in Main.

Stephen Gleasner's wife says he didn't turn 40 right. They had the cake and candles but they also had a seven-month-old baby. So turning 40 was really no big deal. Three years later their second child was born. When he turned 44, Stephen woke in the middle of the night to the realization that he had never raced the Baja 1,000 on a motorcycle. He had no motorcycle and hadn't ridden one in many years. His brain sparked away on this problem. Then he found the Great Divide Mountain bike route. It put a hook in his mouth that he couldn't shake. Two years later he flew from Maine to Banff to race in the first ever Tour Divide Race, promising his wife that his midlife crisis would be over when he got back. He showed up under-trained and over-packed. In the 2008 race he logged more hours in last place than any other racer. When he is not having a midlife crisis, Stephen Gleasner is an artist. He works in plywood. He invented Plyscapes. His works are in collections all over the US and as far away as Hong Kong.

Ward Grovetch lives in New York City. He grew up not far from the Continental Divide and longs to return someday. Ward works at a large trading firm on complex financial instruments which he swears had nothing to do with the current economic meltdown.

Leah Hieber lives in central Washington with her husband Frank and their son Ender. She teaches English.

Paul Howard was born and raised in Yorkshire, England. After a narrow escape from the law (as a profession), he has worked variously as a gardener, field researcher, cave tour guide and journalist. Paul writes regularly for the cycling press as well as for national newspapers (Observer, Guardian, Telegraph, Independent) on cycling and travel. Paul's latest book, about his 2009 Tour Divide race, is called Two Wheels on My Wagon – a Bicycle Adventure in the Wild West (www.mainstreampublishing.com). It is available on Amazon.com. He lives in Sussex with his wife and four children.

Jill Homer is a journalist in Alaska. She first picked up on adventure bicycle racing shortly after moving to Homer, Alaska, in 2005. She was browsing REI one day when she saw a brochure for a 100-mile snow race called the Susitna 100. Despite receiving a mixture of horrified glances and bursts of laughter from everyone she mentioned the race to, she decided to start training. Twenty-five hours and 100 pain-drenched miles later, she was hooked. She competed in that race twice and then moved on to the 350-mile Iditarod Trail Invitational. The Tour Divide was her first "summer" ultra. She finished the 2009 race in 24 days, seven hours and 24 minutes.

Tony Huston is a 37 year old IT professional working for NASA under Lockheed Martin Mission Services. He was born in December of 1972 in southeast Houston, TX, where he still lives today with his wife, Amy, and his daughter, Lauren. He attended South Houston High School, San Jacinto College, and the University of Houston before landing in the aerospace industry in 1998, where he has garnered numerous awards for his contributions to the space program. In quieter times Tony loves reading, writing, working word puzzles, and watching movies. Tony and Amy hope to move to Colorado in the future and open a mountain bike/horse ranch near the Rocky Mountains.

Mark Jenkins is a staff writer for National Geographic Magazine and the author of four books.

Scott Morris runs a website dedicated to bikepacking and self-supported mountain bike racing (http://bikepacking.net) and has been involved with divide racing since 2005. Most recently he is responsible for the 2009/2010 Tour Divide SPOT tracking software. When not bikepacking or racing on the Arizona Trail, he can be found at the computer, working on TopoFusion GPS software or his PhD at the University of Arizona.

Joe Polk is the founder and voice of MTBCast.com which provides audio updates and analysis for endurance bike races including the Iditarod Invitational, Great Divide Race, Tour Divide Race, and the Colorado Trail

Race. Joe works in technology and lives in Sugar Hill, Georgia where he rides some of the sweetest single-track in the country. He also volunteers, doing trail work with a local SORBA chapter in Gainesville, Georgia helping to keep the Chicopee Woods Mountain Bike Trails open for the thousands that visit the park annually.

Glenn Stalgren lives far from the Continental Divide on Martha's Vineyard with his wife Julie, their son Grady and a half crazed dog named Kermit. He can usually be found fishing on the beach, except in June when he's glued to the computer watching the Tour Divide.

John Stamstad is a member of the Mountain Bike Hall of Fame and celebrated endurance athlete. He was the first to time-trial the Great Divide Mountain Bike Route. John is currently focused on long distance running and serves as an "ambassador" for the outdoor equipment manufacturer Patagonia. He lives in Seattle with his wife and three children.

Felix Wong, born in 1975, is a resident of Fort Collins, Colorado with a life-long passion for travel and adventure. He is the second-youngest person ever to complete the California Triple Crown Stage Race at age 23, and is also a veteran of 1200-kilometer Paris-Brest-Paris, the oldest bicycle race in the world. He finished the 2008 Tour Divide in 6th place.

1475455R0

Printed in Great Britain by
Amazon.co.uk, Ltd.,
Marston Gate.